7

TESTAMENT

COLLEGEVILLE BIBLE COMMENTARY

JOSHUA

JUDGES

John A. Grindel, C.M.

D0027162

THE LITURGICAL PRESS

Collegeville, Minnesota

ABBREVIATIONS

Gen—Genesis
Exod—Exodus
Lev—Leviticus
Num—Numbers
Deut—Deuteronomy
Josh—Joshua
Judg—Judges
Ruth—Ruth
1 Sam—1 Samuel
2 Sam—2 Samuel
1 Kgs—1 Kings
2 Kgs—2 Kings
1 Chr—1 Chronicles
2 Chr—2 Chronicles
Ezra—Ezra
Neh—Nehemiah
Tob—Tobit
Jdt—Judith
Esth—Esther
1 Macc—1 Maccabees
2 Macc—2 Maccabees
Job—Job
Ps(s)—Psalm(s)
Prov—Proverbs

Eccl—Ecclesiastes
Song—Song of Songs
Wis—Wisdom
Sir—Sirach
Isa—Isaiah
Jer—Jeremiah
Lam—Lamentations
Bar—Baruch
Ezek—Ezekiel
Dan—Daniel
Hos—Hosea
Joel—Joel
Amos—Amos
Obad—Obadiah
Jonah—Jonah
Mic—Micah
Nah—Nahum
Hab—Habakkuk
Zeph—Zephaniah
Hag—Haggai
Zech—Zechariah
Mal—Malachi
Matt—Matthew
Mark—Mark
Luke—Luke

John—John
Acts—Acts
Rom—Romans
1 Cor—1 Corinthians
2 Cor—2 Corinthians
Gal—Galatians
Eph—Ephesians
Phil—Philippians
Col—Colossians
1 Thess—1 Thessalonians
2 Thess—2 Thessalonians
1 Tim—1 Timothy
2 Tim—2 Timothy
Titus—Titus
Phlm—Philemon
Heb—Hebrews
Jas—James
1 Pet—1 Peter
2 Pet—2 Peter
1 John—1 John
2 John—2 John
3 John—3 John
Jude—Jude
Rev—Revelation

Nihil obstat: Robert C. Harren, J.C.L., *Censor deputatus.*

Imprimatur: ✛ George H. Speltz, D.D., Bishop of St. Cloud, June 18, 1985.

Library of Congress Cataloging in Publication Data

Grindel, John A.
    Joshua, Judges.
    (Collegeville Bible commentary. Old Testament ; 7)
    1. Bible. O.T. Joshua—Commentaries. 2. Bible.
O.T. Judges—Commentaries. I. Title. II. Series.
BS1295.3.G74 1985   222'.2077   85-18194
ISBN 0-8146-1414-0

Cover: Blowing the ram's horn at the Western Wall in Jerusalem. *Photo by Richard T. Nowitz*

CONTENTS

The Book of Joshua

Introduction

The Book of Joshua is named after its chief actor, Joshua, the son of Nun. Joshua had been Moses' aide and succeeded him as the leader of the people. In Hebrew the name Joshua means "Yahweh saves" or "May Yahweh save." The theme of the book is the occupation of the land west of the Jordan River. The book falls into three distinct sections: the conquest of Canaan (chs. 1–12); the division of the land (chs. 13–21); the return of the Transjordan tribes and the farewell of Joshua (chs. 22–24).

The Deuteronomistic History

In the Hebrew Bible the Book of Joshua is the first of what are termed the "former prophets," so called because of the importance of the prophetic word in the books. Today the book is usually seen as the first volume in what is known as the Deuteronomistic History. The Deuteronomistic History includes the Books of Joshua, Judges, Samuel, and Kings, and spans the period from the conquest of Canaan in the twelfth century B.C. down to the time of the Exile in the sixth century B.C. The Book of Deuteronomy is often considered the introduction to these books.

Our modern understanding of the larger Deuteronomistic History owes much to the work of a German scholar, Martin Noth. He was able to show that someone who shared the theological perspective, as well as literary style found in the Book of Deuteronomy, formed a continuous historical work by pulling together into a coherent whole many different units of material which were originally independent and came from various periods of Israel's history. The author drew from numerous written and oral sources, such as annals, kings' lists, and stories of different kinds. Some of the units were of substantial size, such as Josh 2–11. The author's own additions established an interpretative framework that linked the disparate material together and provided judgments on the events in the story. The editor's additions are especially found in punctuating comments—sermons and speeches put into the mouths of important characters at periods of significant transition in the story (e.g., Josh 1 and 24; 1 Sam 12; 1 Kgs 8), bridge passages, and summaries. Scholars debate whether one person produced this work or a school of writers. Most presume that the present edition was composed soon after the last event reported in it, namely, the release of the last Judean king, Jehoiachin, from a Babylonian prison in 561 B.C. Though most believe the work to have been composed in Palestine, others think that it was written in Babylonia.

While Martin Noth thought that there was only one edition of the work, written around 550 B.C., it is more common today to speak of two editions. The earlier first edition was probably written during the reign of King Josiah (620–609 B.C.). The later second edition, which was quite thorough, would have been compiled during the Exile in the sixth century. This commentary will explain the book from the perspective of the second edition, that of the exilic editor.

The Deuteronomistic History was not written just to preserve a memory of the past; rather, its purpose was to give a theological explanation of the loss of the two kingdoms of Israel and Judah, and to provide a theological basis for a hope in the future. To understand the work it is necessary to see it against the background of the times in which it was written.

In 721 B.C. the Assyrians destroyed the northern kingdom of Israel; and in 587 B.C., the Babylonians destroyed the southern kingdom of Judah. When Jerusalem fell in 587 B.C., the city, with its magnificent temple and palace, was leveled, and the leaders of the people were led off into exile in Babylonia.

The period of the Exile was a time of despair and deep questioning on the part of the people. Yahweh had promised to watch over the people, and to protect and guide them; but now all had been lost. Why had the Lord allowed this destruction and the loss of everything? The people especially wondered if they were still the people of God, and if there were any basis for a hope in the future. Would God remain true to the promises made in the past despite all that had happened since? It was in this context that the Deuteronomistic History was written.

The author's purpose is to explain that Israel had lost all because of her sinfulness. The Lord had called the people to fidelity to the covenant, and had warned them of the consequences of infidelity, but the people had sinned. Hence, in exile they were experiencing the divine judgment. Israel had not been faithful to Yahweh, and her long history of sin justified the punishment she was enduring.

The work is also an exhortation to the people to repent and turn back to the Lord and to trust that God will keep the ancient promises. The people are to believe that as God responded positively to repentant people in the past, so will God now hear their cries and forgive them once again. All the ancient promises are still in force, though temporarily suspended because of the sinfulness of the people. At the same time these promises can serve as a basis for the future if the people will only repent.

The purpose of the Book of Joshua

In the context of the Deuteronomistic History the specific purpose of the Book of Joshua, with its emphasis on the conquest and division of the land, is to show the fidelity of God to the promises made in the past to the patriarchs and Moses—particularly the promise of the land. One of the chief themes found in the Pentateuch is the promise of the land. That promise is fulfilled in the Book of Joshua so as to engender in the people a trust in God's promises. Now Israel, in the midst of the Exile, can trust in God's continuing care and presence, and trust especially that the promise of the land remains in force. At the same time, obedience to the Law is important lest, having been forgiven and brought back to the land, Israel again bring down upon her head such destruction as she is now experiencing.

Historical accuracy

A question that is often raised regarding the Book of Joshua is just how accurate is it from a historical perspective, especially in terms of its reporting on the conquest of the land in the twelfth century B.C. This is not an easy question to answer. There are inconsistencies and contradictions in the book itself (compare 4:3 and 4:9; 8:3 and 8:12). What are we to think of the conflicting reports of the conquest of the land found in Josh 1–12 and Judg 1:1–2:5? While the picture presented in Joshua is that of a violent and complete conquest of the land by a united Israel, the picture painted in Judges is that of individual tribes or clans slowly taking their own land and settling down next to the Canaanites in the country. This latter picture is probably closer to the reality.

The author uses different kinds of material in the book, ranging from factual documents to legends. It is also clear that the author, writing over five hundred years after the events being presented, has chosen material so that it would stress a theological viewpoint. In addition, the author has interspersed speeches created out of this theological perspective throughout the work.

Archaeological evidence also raises questions concerning the historical reliability of some of the material in the book, especially the traditions about the cities of Jericho and Ai. While the Book of Joshua gives extensive reports about the conquest of these two cities, archaeological evidence shows that they were not occupied after the fourteenth century B.C., and that Ai had been destroyed about a thousand years before the Israelites entered the land.

In conclusion, then, it is clear that the story, as we have it in the Book of Joshua, is simplified, schematic, incomplete, influenced by the theological views of the author, and the result of compiling very diverse material. We will make some judgments about the historical accuracy of the individual stories as we continue this commentary.

It is interesting to note that most of the material in chapters 1–12 dealing with the conquest of the land seems to be associated with the territory of Benjamin (see ch. 18:11-28) and the sanctuary of Gilgal. It would appear that the traditions in the first part of the book were gathered together and handed on at the sanctuary of Gilgal. The tribal lists in chapters 13–21, on the other hand, all date from the period of the monarchy. While some of the lists incorporated here may go back to the time of David and Solomon in the tenth century, others, such as those in chapters 20 and 21, come from the period of Josiah in the seventh century. One must be careful in accepting too quickly the biblical story of the conquest and the division of the land at face value. The reality was much more complex. We must keep in mind that the author was more interested in bringing out the meaning and significance of the events reported than in reporting exactly what happened. For it is in the meaning of events that one learns of God, oneself, and what God demands of us.

The person and work of Joshua

Against the above background on the historical reliability of the material in the Book of Joshua the person and work of Joshua also becomes a problem. If one accepts the view presented in the Deuteronomistic History that the conquest was the result of a united military action, then Joshua, as the supreme commander of the Israelite forces, plays an important role. But when we know the conquest to have been a century-long process of internal revolution, slow infiltration, and occupation by individual groups, then the figure of Joshua is difficult to explain. What adds to the problem is that while the traditions of the conquest preserved in the Book of Joshua are from the tribe of Benjamin, Joshua was from the tribe of Ephraim.

What all of this shows is that the very complicated history of the conquest has been reduced in the Book of Joshua to a small group of typical stories which are now attributed to all Israel, but which originally came primarily from the traditions of the tribe of Benjamin. These exploits have now been attributed to Joshua, a well-known person who had been active either militarily or in resolving conflicts in the central hill country of Palestine.

The Book of Joshua

Text and Commentary

I: CONQUEST OF CANAAN

1 **Divine Promise of Assistance.** ¹After Moses, the servant of the LORD, had died, the LORD said to Moses' aide Joshua, son of Nun: ²"My servant Moses is dead. So prepare to cross the Jordan here, with all the people, into the land I will give the Israelites. ³As I promised Moses, I will deliver to you every place where you set foot. ⁴Your domain is to be all the land of the Hittites, from the desert and from Lebanon east to the great river Euphrates and west to the Great Sea. ⁵No one can withstand you while you live. I will be

PART I: THE CONQUEST OF CANAAN

Josh 1:1–12:24

1:1–2:24 Preparations. The book begins with a report on the preparations for entrance into the land of Canaan. First, there is the Lord's commissioning of Joshua (1:1-9), which is followed by Joshua's orders to the people (1:10-18) and the sending of spies across the river to reconnoiter the land, especially Jericho (2:1-24).

1:1-9 The commissioning of Joshua. This passage, like all of chapter 1, comes from the hand of the Deuteronomistic Historian (henceforth D) and forms the transition from the death of Moses (see Deut 34) to the conquest of the land. The passage picks up on and develops the original commissioning of Joshua in Deut 31. In sermon style the passage follows the formula for the divine installation of a person into public office: a description of the task to be performed, an expression of encouragement, and an assurance of divine assistance. Joshua is presented as the successor to Moses with the command to complete his work.

The task that is given to Joshua is to lead the people into the land that the Lord will give to the Israelites. From the beginning (v. 2) it is made clear that the land is a gift of the Lord to the people; it is not something that they have earned. The granting of this gift is the fulfillment of the promise to Moses (v. 3). The description of the boundaries of the land in verse 4 is the most comprehensive description of the land found anywhere in the Bible. There are three fixed points in this description: the "desert," which refers to the Negeb in the south and the area east of the Jordan River; the "Euphrates," which describes the northeastern boundary; and the "Great Sea," which describes the Mediterranean on the west. As defined here the land included

with you as I was with Moses: I will not leave you nor forsake you. ⁶Be firm and steadfast, so that you may give this people possession of the land which I swore to their fathers I would give them. ⁷Above all, be firm and steadfast, taking care to observe the entire law which my servant Moses enjoined on you. Do not swerve from it either to the right or to the left, that you may succeed wherever you go. ⁸Keep this book of the law on your lips. Recite it by day and by night, that you may observe carefully all that is written in it; then you will successfully attain your goal. ⁹I command you: be firm and steadfast! Do not fear nor be dismayed, for the LORD, your God, is with you wherever you go."

¹⁰So Joshua commanded the officers of the people: ¹¹"Go through the camp and instruct the people, 'Prepare your provisions, for three days from now you shall cross the Jordan here, to march in and take possession of the land which the LORD, your God, is giving you.'"

The Transjordan Tribes. ¹²Joshua reminded the Reubenites, the Gadites, and the half-tribe of Manasseh: ¹³"Remember what Moses, the servant of the LORD, commanded you when he said, The LORD, your God, will permit you to settle in this land.' ¹⁴Your wives, your children, and your livestock shall remain in the land Moses gave you here beyond the Jordan. But all the warriors among you must cross over armed ahead of your kinsmen and you must help them ¹⁵until the LORD has settled your kinsmen, and

the area of Lebanon to the northwest and almost the whole of present-day and ancient Syria. However, these boundaries were never a reality. The only time Israel even began to have such extensive boundaries was in the time of David and Solomon in the tenth century. Joshua will be able to fulfill the promise because of the Lord's presence with him (v. 5).

Though the land is a gift of the Lord, verses 6-9 insist upon the necessity of Israel being "firm and steadfast," i.e., observing all that is written in the law in order to attain possession of the land. In other words, Israel's disobedience can frustrate the divine promises. All of this is an important message for the exiles who can hear in this passage both the reason for the loss of the land (their disobedience) and the conditions for regaining the land (obedience to the law, trust in the Lord, and the Lord's promises of presence).

1:10-18 Joshua's orders to the people. Having received the Lord's instructions, Joshua now gives orders that the people are to be instructed to prepare provisions, because in three days they are to march in and take possession of the land that the Lord is giving them (vv. 10-11). Notice how the conquest is described as something peaceful, almost like a cultic procession. It is as if the Lord has already decreed that Israel will possess the land and now the people need only to carry it out.

In verses 12-15 Joshua reminds the tribes who have already settled in the area east of the Jordan River of the command of Moses (see Deut 3:12-20) that all the warriors from these tribes must help their kinspeople to settle in the land across the Jordan before they can return to their own land. The conquest must be seen as a unified undertaking by Israel.

they like you possess the land which the LORD, your God, is giving them. Afterward you may return and occupy your own land, which Moses, the servant of the LORD, has given you east of the Jordan." ¹⁶"We will do all you have commanded us," they answered Joshua, "and we will go wherever you send us. We will obey you as completely as we obeyed Moses. ¹⁷But may the LORD, your God, be with you as he was with Moses. ¹⁸If anyone rebels against your orders and does not obey every command you give him, he shall be put to death. But be firm and steadfast."

2 Spies Saved by Rahab. ¹Then Joshua, son of Nun, secretly sent out two spies from Shittim, saying, "Go, reconnoiter the land and Jericho." When the two reached Jericho, they went into the house of a harlot named Rahab, where they lodged. ²But a report was brought to the king of Jericho that some Israelites had come there that night to spy out the land. ³So the king of Jericho sent Rahab the order, "Put out the visitors who have entered your house, for they have come to spy out the entire land." ⁴The woman had taken the two men and hidden them,

so she said, "True, the men you speak of came to me, but I did not know where they came from. ⁵At dark, when it was time for the gate to be shut, they left, and I do not know where they went. You will have to pursue them immediately to overtake them." ⁶Now, she had led them to the roof, and hidden them among her stalks of flax spread out there. ⁷But the pursuers set out along the way to the fords of the Jordan, and once they had left, the gate was shut.

⁸Before the spies fell asleep, Rahab came to them on the roof ⁹and said: "I know that the LORD has given you the land, that a dread of you has come upon us, and that all the inhabitants of the land are overcome with fear of you. ¹⁰For we have heard how the LORD dried up the waters of the Red Sea before you when you came out of Egypt, and how you dealt with Sihon and Og, the two kings of the Amorites beyond the Jordan, whom you doomed to destruction. ¹¹At these reports, we are disheartened; everyone is discouraged because of you, since the LORD, your God, is God in heaven above and on earth below. ¹²Now then, swear to me by the LORD that, since

Verses 16-18 present the response of the Transjordanian tribes. They will do all that Joshua commands as long as they are assured of the presence of the Lord with him (vv. 16-17). The main purpose of these verses is to show the acceptance of the transfer of leadership from Moses to Joshua.

2:1-24 Reconnaissance of Jericho. The attentive reader will notice immediately the tension between this chapter and the material in chapters 1 and 3. First of all, the location of the Israelite camp is now said to be at Shittim, which is probably the Abel-shittim mentioned in Num 33:49.

Secondly, the chronology of this chapter is incompatible with that of chapters 1 and 3. Chapter 1 speaks of three days as the interval between Joshua's orders to the people and the actual entrance into the land (see v. 11). However, the present story says that the spies spent three days in the hills before returning to the Israelite camp (2:22), not to mention the time spent going to Jericho and returning. Also, verses 1 and 2 of chapter 3 seem to flow directly after 1:18.

I am showing kindness to you, you in turn will show kindness to my family; and give me an unmistakable token ¹³that you are to spare my father and mother, brothers and sisters, and all their kin, and save us from death." ¹⁴"We pledge our lives for yours," the men answered her. "If you do not betray this errand of ours, we will be faithful in showing kindness to you when the LORD gives us the land."

¹⁵Then she let them down through the window with a rope; for she lived in a house built into the city wall. ¹⁶"Go up into the hill country," she suggested to them, "that your pursuers may not find you. Hide there for three days, until they return; then you may proceed on your way." ¹⁷The men answered her, "This is how we will fulfill the oath you made us take: ¹⁸When we come into the land, tie this scarlet cord in the window through which you are letting us down; and gather your father and mother, your brothers and all your family into your house. ¹⁹Should any of them pass outside the doors of your house, he will be responsible for his own death, and we shall be guiltless. But we shall be responsible if anyone in the house with you is harmed. ²⁰If, however, you betray this errand of ours, we shall be quit of the oath you have made us take." ²¹"Let it be as you say," she replied, and bade them farewell. When they were gone, she tied the scarlet cord in the window.

²²They went up into the hills, where they stayed three days until their pursuers, who had sought them all along the road without finding them, returned. ²³Then the two came back down from the hills, crossed the Jordan to Joshua, son of Nun, and reported all that had befallen them. ²⁴They assured Joshua, "The LORD has delivered all this land into our power; indeed, all the inhabitants of the land are overcome with fear of us."

Finally, one encounters a different style in the present story from the style of the material in chapters 1 and 3. All of this means that this present story undoubtedly was a later insertion into the narrative. In fact there are indications that the story of Rahab is quite old and possibly goes back to the time before David. It appears that D has used the story as it was found, with the possible exception of Rahab's profession of faith in verses 9-11. This profession of faith reflects Deuteronomic themes (compare to Deut 26:5b-9 and Josh 24:2b-13).

In its original form the story of Rahab and the spies was probably an etiological tale, i.e., a narrative that explained something by giving the story of its origins. What the story explained was the survival of the Canaanite family of Rahab in the midst of the Israelites after the conquest. In its present context, however, the interest of the author is in Rahab's profession of faith. Through Rahab's profession D is emphasizing that it is the Lord who is responsible for all that is about to take place. The one who is God in heaven above and on earth below has given the land to Israel and with power will now lead them into the land. D is attempting to instill hope in the exiles by reminding them of who their God is. If the Lord could act like this in the past, then that same Lord can act with power on their behalf now.

3 Preparations for Crossing the Jordan. ¹Early the next morning, Joshua moved with all the Israelites from Shittim to the Jordan, where they lodged before crossing over. ²Three days later the officers went through the camp ³and issued these instructions to the people: "When you see the ark of the covenant of the LORD, your God, which the levitical priests will carry, you must also break camp and follow it, ⁴that you may know the way to take, for you have not gone over this road before. But let there be a space of two thousand cubits between you and the ark. Do not come nearer to it." ⁵Joshua also said to the people, "Sanctify yourselves, for tomorrow the LORD will perform wonders among you." ⁶And he directed the priests to take up the ark of the covenant and go on ahead of the people; and they did so.

⁷Then the LORD said to Joshua, "Today I will begin to exalt you in the sight of all Israel, that they may know I am with you, as I was with Moses. ⁸Now command the priests carrying the ark of the covenant to come to a halt in the Jordan when they reach the edge of the waters."

3:1–5:12 The crossing of the Jordan. Having dealt with the preparations for entering the land, the author narrates the crossing of the Jordan. What is found in this section is a series of events that lack internal unity but are held together by their concern with the crossing and with the ark of the covenant. This is the only place where the ark is mentioned in the conquest narrative. The crossing falls into five scenes: preparations (3:1-13); the crossing (3:14-17); the setting up of memorial stones (4:1-9); the completion of the crossing (4:10-18); and the cultic encampment at Gilgal (4:19–5:12).

3:1-13 Preparations. This narrative, along with the narrative of the crossing, presents the event as a solemn liturgical procession. More than likely the story developed as a cultic reenactment and memorial of the crossing of the Jordan. The author has taken this ancient liturgy and used it as an outline for the story, mainly to show that it was the living God, the Lord of the whole earth, who was responsible for bringing Israel into the land (vv. 10-11). Once again an important message is here for the Israelites, namely, that the Lord is powerful and can bring the exiles back to the land as the Lord once before had brought the people into the land.

The text in verses 1 and 2 follows more from 1:18 than from chapter 2. Verses 2-6 point out that it is Yahweh who leads the people. The ark is a sign of the Lord's presence. The distance that people are to keep from the ark emphasizes the respect that one must show the Lord. The call to holiness in verse 5 flows from the idea that the people are about to experience wonders performed by the Lord, i.e., extraordinary actions. Such a divine intervention requires adequate human preparation. Involved in this sanctification is a series of purification rites and abstinence from all sexual activity and certain foods (see Exod 19:10-15; Num 11:18; Josh 7:13).

Verse 7 presents the purpose of the action to follow: it is to exalt Joshua in the sight of all Israel and to confirm his role as the successor of Moses.

⁹So Joshua said to the Israelites, "Come here and listen to the words of the LORD, your God." ¹⁰He continued: "This is how you will know that there is a living God in your midst, who at your approach will dispossess the Canaanites, Hittites, Hivites, Perizzites, Girgashites, Amorites and Jebusites. ¹¹The ark of the covenant of the LORD of the whole earth will precede you into the Jordan. ¹²[Now choose twelve men, one from each of the tribes of Israel.] ¹³When the soles of the feet of the priests carrying the ark of the LORD, the LORD of the whole earth, touch the water of the Jordan, it will cease to flow; for the water flowing down from upstream will halt in a solid bank."

The Crossing Begun. ¹⁴The people struck their tents to cross the Jordan, with the priests carrying the ark of the covenant ahead of them. ¹⁵No sooner had these priestly bearers of the ark waded into the waters at the edge of the Jordan, which overflows all its banks during the entire season of the harvest, ¹⁶than the waters flowing from upstream halted, backing up in a solid mass for a very great distance indeed, from Adam, a city in the direction of Zarethan; while those flowing downstream toward the Salt Sea of the Arabah disappeared entirely. Thus the people crossed over opposite Jericho. ¹⁷While all Israel crossed over on dry ground, the priests carrying the ark of the covenant of the LORD remained motionless on dry ground in the bed of the Jordan until the whole nation had completed the passage.

What will happen will show the presence of the Lord with Joshua. Joshua's sermon in verses 10-13 states who is responsible for what is about to happen—the living God who is the Lord of the whole earth. It is this Lord who will bring the waters to a halt so that the people can cross over. Verse 10 lists the indigenous population of the land in standard form: the Canaanites are found in the coastal cities; the Hittites in small colonies here and there; the Hivites around Shechem and Gibeon; the Amorites inhabited the hill country; and the Jebusites lived in Jerusalem. It is not clear who the Perizzites and Girgashites were.

3:14-17 The crossing. Everything happens now as foretold. In solemn procession the people follow the priests carrying the ark of the covenant and, when the waters halt, the people cross. The crossing is consciously presented as a parallel to the crossing of the Red Sea, because the entrance into the Promised Land is, in a sense, the conclusion of the Lord's great act of deliverance that began with the Exodus. One sees here how the Exodus becomes the prism through which all of God's great acts of deliverance are seen. The return from the Exile will also be seen as a new Exodus. To heighten the sense of the miraculous and the greatness of God's activity, it is made clear that it is late winter or early spring, when the Jordan overflows its banks because of melting snow from the mountains to the north. The river halts at "Adam," a city at the junction of the Jabbok and the Jordan Rivers, several miles north of Jericho. The Salt Sea refers to the Dead Sea, and the Arabah is the desert south of the Dead Sea. The people cross over opposite Jericho. There are several known times when the Jordan has been dammed up for

4 **Memorial Stones.** ¹After the entire nation had crossed the Jordan, the LORD said to Joshua, ²"Choose twelve men from the people, one from each tribe, ³and instruct them to take up twelve stones from this spot in the bed of the Jordan where the priests have been standing motionless. Carry them over with you, and place them where you are to stay tonight."

Summoning the twelve men whom he had selected from among the Israelites, one from each tribe, ⁵Joshua said to them: "Go to the bed of the Jordan in front of the ark of the LORD, your God; lift to your shoulders one stone apiece, so that they will equal in number the tribes of the Israelites. ⁶In the future, these are to be a sign among you. When your children ask you what these stones mean to you, ⁷you shall answer them, 'The waters of the Jordan ceased to flow before the ark of the covenant of the LORD when it crossed the Jordan.' Thus these stones are to serve as a perpetual memorial to the Israelites." ⁸The twelve Israelites did as Joshua had commanded: they took up as many stones from the bed of the Jordan as there were tribes of the Israelites, and carried them along to the camp site, where they placed them, according to the LORD's direction. ⁹Joshua also had twelve stones set up in the bed of the Jordan on the spot where the priests stood who were carrying the ark of the covenant. They are there to this day.

a period of hours because its banks collapsed and formed a natural dam. Perhaps such an event stands behind this story.

4:1-9 The memorial stones. The present episode is a secondary insertion into the text. This is clear from the summary statement in 4:10, which refers back to the crossing in 3:14-17, and from the special interest in the twelve stones at Gilgal. Though the actual location of Gilgal is unknown, it is somewhere in the area of Jericho. From a very early period it was an Israelite national shrine. More than likely it was the natural presence of a group of stones at this sanctuary, later linked to the crossing of the Jordan, that gave rise to this episode. The stones were understood to be a physical reminder, a perpetual memorial (v. 7), of how "the waters of the Jordan ceased to flow before the ark of the covenant of the Lord when it crossed the Jordan." The episode, then, originated as an etiological tale, like the story of Rahab in chapter 2. In these verses two traditions are combined: one that explains the presence of the stones at Gilgal (vv. 1-8) and one that explains the presence of stones in the middle of the Jordan River (v. 9). It is unclear where the latter tradition came from and why it is included in verse 9.

In the present context these verses are meant to emphasize that it was the Lord who brought the Israelites across the Jordan. For the exiles this is a message of hope: this same Lord can bring the exiles back into the land. The explanation of the twelve stones in verse 17 is the midpoint of the whole block of material in 3:1–5:12. The inclusion of this episode may also be an attempt at a further assimilation of the crossing of the Jordan to the tradition of the Exodus-Sinai event (compare with the twelve stones for the twelve tribes of Israel commemorating the covenant at Sinai in Exod 24:4).

15

¹⁰The priests carrying the ark remained in the bed of the Jordan until everything had been done that the LORD had commanded Joshua to tell the people. The people crossed over quickly, ¹¹and when all had reached the other side, the ark of the LORD, borne by the priests, also crossed to its place in front of them. ¹²The Reubenites, Gadites, and half-tribe of Manasseh, armed, marched in the vanguard of the Israelites, as Moses had ordered. ¹³About forty thousand troops equipped for battle passed over before the LORD to the plains of Jericho.

¹⁴That day the LORD exalted Joshua in the sight of all Israel, and thenceforth during his whole life they respected him as they had respected Moses. ¹⁵Then the LORD said to Joshua, ¹⁶"Command the priests carrying the ark of the commandments to come up from the Jordan." ¹⁷Joshua did so, ¹⁸and when the priests carrying the ark of the covenant of the LORD had come up from the bed of the Jordan, as the soles of their feet regained the dry ground, the waters of the Jordan resumed their course and as before overflowed all its banks.

4:10-18 Completion of the crossing. Though these verses seem jumbled, there is a certain logic to them. The condition of the text here is the result of several editors dealing with various concerns. After the insertion of 4:1-9, verse 10 returns the reader to the main narrative by summarizing 3:14-17. Verse 11 is a summary in advance of the exit of the ark from the river. In this liturgical procession the people, having safely crossed the river, now line up to witness the ark being brought out of the river.

Verses 12-13 are an addition by D, who wishes to emphasize here, as in 1:12ff., that all the tribes of Israel were involved—even those who had been granted land east of the Jordan. The number of forty thousand is certainly an exaggeration. Perhaps the solution is that the word that can be translated as "thousand" can also be used as a technical term to indicate a military unit of considerable size.

Verse 14 returns to 3:7 and stresses the major purpose of this miraculous crossing, namely, to exalt Joshua before all Israel. This purpose was accomplished by the great miracle; henceforth, the people respected Joshua as they had Moses. With all the goals of the miracle accomplished, the priests now come up from the river and, as soon as they hit dry ground, the Jordan resumes its course and once again overflows its banks.

4:19-5:12 Cultic encampment at Gilgal. With the crossing of the Jordan, one period in the life of Israel is about to end and another to begin. This section, with its emphasis on various cultic rites at Gilgal, forms the transition from the period of deliverance to the occupation of the land. The section is framed by two cultic events that explicitly refer back to the deliverance from Egypt: the actual setting up of the stones at Gilgal (4:20-24), and the celebration of the Passover (5:10-12). The narrative in 5:1 shows the impact of Israel's entrance into the land on the inhabitants of the area.

¹⁹The people came up from the Jordan on the tenth day of the first month, and camped in Gilgal on the eastern limits of Jericho. ²⁰At Gilgal Joshua set up the twelve stones which had been taken from the Jordan, ²¹saying to the Israelites, "In the future, when the children among you ask their fathers what these stones mean, ²²you shall inform them, 'Israel crossed the Jordan here on dry ground.' ²³For the LORD, your God, dried up the waters of the Jordan in front of you until you crossed over, just as the LORD, your God, had done at the Red Sea, which he dried up in front of us until we crossed over; ²⁴in order that all the peoples of the earth may learn that the hand of the LORD is mighty, and that you may fear the LORD, your God, forever."

5 Rites at Gilgal.
¹When all the kings of the Amorites to the west of the Jordan and all the kings of the Canaanites by the sea heard that the LORD had dried up the waters of the Jordan before the Israelites until they crossed over, they were disheartened and lost courage at their approach.

²On this occasion the LORD said to Joshua, "Make flint knives and circumcise the Israelite nation for the second time." ³So Joshua made flint knives and circumcised the Israelites at Gibeath-

The circumcision of all males, reported in 5:2-9, is to prepare for the celebration of the Passover.

The scene is set in 4:19. The date is the tenth day of the first month, known as Nisan. This is the time of the harvest in March-April. The date is important in view of the celebration of the Passover, which is soon to follow. The place where the people camp after crossing the Jordan is explicitly identified for the first time; it is at Gilgal, here located on the eastern limits of Jericho.

In the story of the memorial stones (4:20-24), it is the explanation of the stones that is important. Notice the explicit comparison of the drying up of the waters of the Jordan to the drying up of the Red Sea (see Exod 14:21). The two events provide the beginning and ending points of the period of deliverance. With the entrance into the land, Israel has achieved the goal for which she was delivered from Egypt (see Exod 3:8). The purpose of the Lord's actions is explicit: that all the people of the earth might learn of the might of God, and that the Israelites might fear the Lord. This is an important message for the exiles: in the midst of their pain they must put hope in the power of their God, and give their full allegiance to the Lord who can deliver.

The point of 5:1 is to show that the Lord's purpose has been achieved among the kings in the land of Canaan. They have recognized the might of the Lord in the events of the crossing and have become "disheartened"; literally, "their hearts melted." See the same term used by Rahab (2:10-11) and in Exod 15:13-17, which narrates the results of the Exodus. Once again the author parallels the crossing of the Jordan and the crossing of the Red Sea.

The story of the circumcision in 5:2-9 is placed here more for theological reasons than for historical ones. Exod 12:48 explains that only the circum-

haaraloth, ⁴under these circumstances: Of all the people who came out of Egypt, every man of military age had died in the desert during the journey after they left Egypt. ⁵Though all the men who came out were circumcised, none of those born in the desert during the journey after the departure from Egypt were circumcised. ⁶Now the Israelites had wandered forty years in the desert, until all the warriors among the people that came forth from Egypt died off because they had not obeyed the command of the LORD. For the LORD swore that he would not let them see the land flowing with milk and honey which he had promised their fathers he would give us. ⁷It was the children whom he raised up in their stead whom Joshua circumcised, for these were yet with foreskins, not having been circumcised on the journey. ⁸When the rite had been performed, the whole nation remained in camp where they were, until they recovered. ⁹Then theLORD said to Joshua, "Today I have removed the reproach of Egypt from you." Therefore the place is called Gilgal to the present day.

¹⁰While the Israelites were encamped at Gilgal on the plains of Jericho, they celebrated the Passover on the evening of the fourteenth of the month. ¹¹On the day after the Passover they ate of the produce of the land in the form of unleavened cakes and parched grain. On that same day ¹²after the Passover on which they ate of the produce of the land, the manna

cised can take part in the celebration of the Passover. For whatever reason (the text gives none), however, the children who were born in the desert during the forty years of wandering since leaving Egypt had not been circumcised. Hence, for a proper celebration of the Passover, circumcision is now necessary. The reference to circumcision taking place for a "second time" (v. 2) intends to show the circumcision and celebration of the Passover at Gilgal as a repetition of the rites surrounding the Exodus (see Exod 12). The site of the ritual is called Gibeath-haaraloth, which means "Hill of the Foreskins," referring to a place near Gilgal where the rite of circumcision was practiced. Notice D's need to explain the reason for the death of all the warriors who had come out of Egypt (see Num 14), probably to explain to the exiles why they had lost their land, namely, because of their disobedience. In verse 9 an attempt is made to explain the name Gilgal. The place is so named because here the Lord "removed," literally, "rolled away" the reproach of Israel. One of the meanings that the root of the word "gilgal" can have is "to roll away." It is not clear what is meant by the "reproach of Egypt."

The section concludes with the celebration of the Passover (vv. 10-12), the festival celebrating the Exodus. The fourteenth day of the first month was the proper date for this celebration (see Exod 12:1-6). As the Exodus began with the celebration of the Passover, so the entrance into the land, which brings this period of deliverance to an end, concludes with the same celebration. The next day the people eat of the produce of the land, and with this event the manna (see Exod 16 and Deut 8:3) ceases, since there is no longer a need for it. It is truly the end of an era.

eased. No longer was there manna for the Israelites, who that year ate of the yield of the land of Canaan.

Siege at Jericho. ¹³While Joshua was near Jericho, he raised his eyes and saw one who stood facing him, drawn sword in hand. Joshua went up to him and asked, "Are you one of us or of our enemies?" ¹⁴He replied, "Neither. I am the captain of the host of the LORD and I have just arrived." Then Joshua fell prostrate to the ground in worship, and said to him, "What has my lord to say to his servant?" ¹⁵The captain of the host of the LORD replied to Joshua, "Remove your sandals from your feet, for the place on

which you are standing is holy." And Joshua obeyed.

6 ¹Now Jericho was in a state of siege because of the presence of the Israelites, so that no one left or entered. ²And to Joshua the LORD said, "I have delivered Jericho and its king into your power. ³Have all the soldiers circle the city, marching once around it. Do this for six days, ⁴with seven priests carrying ram's horns ahead of the ark. On the seventh day march around the city seven times, and have the priests blow the horns. ⁵When they give a long blast on the ram's horns and you hear that signal, all the people shall shout aloud. The wall

5:13–12:24 The conquest. These chapters contain the narrative of the conquest: the conquest of the central part of the land (5:13–9:27); the conquest of the south (10:1-43); and the conquest of the north (11:1-15). The concluding verses (11:16–12:24) present a summary.

5:13–9:27 The conquest of the center of the land. These chapters narrate the capture of Jericho (5:13–6:27), the defeat and victory at Ai (7:1–8:29), the altar on Mount Ebal (8:30-35), and the Gibeonite alliance (9:1-27).

5:13–6:27 The capture of Jericho. The story begins with the apparition of a divine being that recalls Exod 3, the call of Moses. Joshua is to be understood as the new Moses. Though the material in 5:13-15 probably belonged originally to an independent epic, it now forms a unit with 6:1-5, which tells of the Lord's pronouncement of the fall of Jericho and instructions on how the city is to be taken. The presence of the captain of the host of the Lord shows the presence of the Lord in the conquest, right from the beginning. As 6:2 brings out, it is the Lord who is responsible for the fall of Jericho. The trumpets made of rams' horns (6:4) were commonly used in warfare and liturgies.

Archaeological evidence shows that Jericho was already in ruins when the Israelites entered into Canaan. Any habitation of the site of Tell es-Sultan, the site identified as Jericho, was sparse at the time of the conquest. What gave rise to the belief that it had been destroyed in the conquest was the fact that the site had lain in ruins in the period of the Judges and on into the period of the monarchy. Being close to the national sanctuary of Gilgal, the presupposition arose of its destruction under Joshua. Historically, it is not possible to say what lies behind the present narrative.

19

of the city will collapse, and they will be able to make a frontal attack."

⁶Summoning the priests, Joshua, son of Nun, then ordered them to take up the ark of the covenant with seven of the priests carrying ram's horns in front of the ark of the LORD. ⁷And he ordered the people to proceed in a circle around the city, with the picked troops marching ahead of the ark of the LORD. ⁸At this order they proceeded, with the seven priests who carried the ram's horns before the LORD blowing their horns, and the ark of the covenant of the LORD following them. ⁹In front of the priests with the horns marched the picked troops; the rear-guard followed the ark, and the blowing of horns was kept up continually as they marched. ¹⁰But the people had been commanded by Joshua not to shout or make any noise or outcry until he gave the word: only then were they to shout. ¹¹So he had the ark of the LORD circle the city, going once around it, after which they returned to camp for the night. ¹²Early the next morning, Joshua had the priests take up the ark of the LORD. ¹³The seven priests bearing the ram's horns marched in front of the ark of the LORD, blowing their horns. Ahead of these marched the picked troops, while the rear-guard followed the ark of the LORD, and the blowing of horns was kept up continually. ¹⁴On this second day they again marched around the city once before returning to camp; and for six days in all they did the same.

¹⁵On the seventh day, beginning at daybreak, they marched around the city seven times in the same manner; on that day only did they march around the city seven times. ¹⁶The seventh time around, the priests blew the horns and Joshua said to the people, "Now shout, for the LORD has given you the city ¹⁷and everything in it. It is under the LORD's ban. Only the harlot Rahab and all who are in the house with her are to be spared, because she hid the messengers we sent. ¹⁸But be careful not to take, in your greed, anything that is under the ban; else you will bring upon the camp of Israel this ban and the misery of it. ¹⁹All silver and gold, and the articles of bronze or iron, are sacred to the LORD. They shall be put in the treasury of the LORD."

The Fall of Jericho. ²⁰As the horns blew, the people began to shout. When

The narrative in chapter 6 is quite complicated and seems to have gone through various editions. In its final form the story has the characteristics of a religious ritual, a liturgy. D wants to stress to the exiles that it was Yahweh who was responsible for the conquest of the land and that same Yahweh can once again lead them to victory. This first success in Canaan takes on a symbolic value of the power of the Lord. The multiple use of the number seven, a sacred number in Israel, plays up the presence of the Lord in this narrative.

Having received instructions from the Lord on how to go about the conquest of Jericho, Joshua passes them on to the priests and people. These orders are executed and the city falls before the Israelites (6:12-21). The point of the "ban" in verses 17ff. is that since the Lord is the warrior and the victor, the enemy and booty belong to the Lord. Hence, they are sacred and taboo. To approach too close is to approach too close to God. To destroy such is an act of devotion to the Lord.

The Jordan River, which the Israelites miraculously crossed to occupy Canaan (Josh 3:1–4:24). Photo by Makoto Tada, O.S.B.

Excavation at Jericho, the first city captured from the Canaanites by Joshua and the Israelites. Photo by Hugh Witzmann, O.S.B.

they heard the signal horn, they raised a tremendous shout. The wall collapsed, and the people stormed the city in a frontal attack and took it. ²¹They observed the ban by putting to the sword all living creatures in the city: men and women, young and old, as well as oxen, sheep and asses.

²²Joshua directed the two men who had spied out the land, "Go into the harlot's house and bring out the woman with all her kin, as you swore to her you would do." ²³The spies entered and brought out Rahab, with her father, mother, brothers, and all her kin. Her entire family they led forth and placed them outside the camp of Israel. ²⁴The city itself they burned with all that was in it, except the silver, gold, and articles of bronze and iron, which were placed in the treasury of the house of the LORD. ²⁵Because Rahab the harlot had hidden the messengers whom Joshua had sent to reconnoiter Jericho, Joshua spared her with her family and all her kin, who continue in the midst of Israel to this day.

²⁶On that occasion Joshua imposed the oath: Cursed before the LORD be the man who attempts to rebuild this city, Jericho. He shall lose his first-born when he lays its foundation, and he shall lose his youngest son when he sets up its gates. ²⁷Thus the LORD was with Joshua so that his fame spread throughout the land.

Verses 22-25, along with the reference to Rahab in verse 17, are probably an addition to help tie the story of the fall of Jericho to the story of Rahab in chapter 2. These verses conclude the etiology begun in chapter 2 that explains the presence of Rahab and her family in the midst of Israel. The mention of the treasury of the house of the Lord in verse 24 is often understood to refer to the temple of Jerusalem, which had not yet been built! More likely, it refers to the sanctuary at Gilgal.

The narrative of the fall of Jericho seems to recall memories of a military conquest on the basis of a ruse (6:1, 20, 21, 25). These may well be ancient memories of the original fall of the city. The curse, which is reported in 6:26, explains why the city was not rebuilt, and finds its fulfillment in 1 Kgs 16:34. (One of these texts depends upon the other, but it is not clear which way the dependency goes.)

7:1–8:29 Defeat and victory at Ai. The material in chapters 7 and 8 is composed of at least two narratives that were combined, probably before the time of D. The main story told of an original defeat of Israel at Ai. To this has been combined an ancient story of the crime and punishment of Achan in order to give an explanation of the defeat. The only difficulty with the combined narrative is that at the time of the Israelite conquest, Ai (today identified as et-Tell) was uninhabited. Archaeological evidence shows that the city was last inhabited at the end of the third millennium and not settled again until the eleventh century. Several theories have been advanced to explain the present narrative. One prominent theory says that the story originally described the fall of Bethel, which is only a couple of miles away, and was later connected with the ruins at et-Tell. The basis for this theory

7 Defeat at Ai. ¹But the Israelites violated the ban; Achan, son of Carmi, son of Zerah, son of Zara of the tribe of Judah, took goods that were under the ban, and the anger of the LORD flared up against the Israelites.

²Joshua next sent men from Jericho to Ai, which is near Bethel on its eastern side, with instructions to go up and reconnoiter the land. When they had explored Ai, ³they returned to Joshua and advised, "Do not send all the people up; if only about two or three thousand go up, they can overcome Ai. The enemy there are few; you need not call for an effort from all the people." ⁴About three thousand of the people made the attack, but they were defeated by those at Ai, ⁵who killed some thirty-six of them. They pressed them back across the clearing in front of the city gate till they broke ranks, and defeated them finally on the descent, so that the confidence of the people melted away like water.

⁶Joshua, together with the elders of Israel, rent his garments and lay prostrate before the ark of the LORD until evening; and they threw dust on their heads. ⁷"Alas, O Lord GOD," Joshua prayed, "why did you ever allow this people to pass over the Jordan, delivering us into the power of the Amorites, that they might destroy us? Would that we had been content to dwell on the other side of the Jordan. ⁸Pray, Lord, what can I say, now that Israel has turned its back to its enemies? ⁹When the Canaanites and the other inhabitants of the land hear of

is the archaeological evidence, which shows that Bethel was destroyed toward the end of the thirteenth century. However, it is not clear that this destruction was due to the Israelites. Though the real source of the story is unknown, it is evident that both narratives are quite old. As we shall see, the major thrust of the combined narratives is to show to the exiles that a violation of the covenant leads to defeat and destruction, while faith and obedience lead to victory.

The author begins (v. 1) by explaining that the Lord was angry with Israel because Achan had violated the ban (see 6:18); hence, there should be no surprise at the defeat that is about to take place. Here is introduced the idea of corporate guilt, i.e., how the whole people could suffer because of the sin of one person.

Notice that nothing is said in verses 2-3 of the Lord's involvement. All is being done at the initiative of Israel. Hence, when Israel attacks she is defeated and the confidence of the people melts away (vv. 4-5). The word used here for "thousands" probably refers to a military contingent of some size.

Joshua with the elders now consults the Lord (vv. 6-9). Joshua's real concern is expressed in verse 9, namely, that when the other inhabitants of the land hear of the defeat, they will turn on Israel. The rites described in these verses pertain to the ritual of mourning (see Deut 9:26; Exod 32:11; 2 Sam 12:15-17). The passage recalls Israel's complaints against Moses and the Lord when they were in the desert (see Exod 16:2-8).

23

it, they will close in around us and efface our name from the earth. What will you do for your great name?" ¹⁰The LORD replied to Joshua: "Stand up. Why are you lying prostrate? ¹¹Israel has sinned: they have violated the covenant which I enjoined on them. They have stealthily taken goods subject to the ban, and have deceitfully put them in their baggage. ¹²If the Israelites cannot stand up to their enemies, but must turn their back to them, it is because they are under the ban. I will not remain with you unless you remove from among you whoever has incurred the ban. ¹³Rise, sanctify the people. Tell them to sanctify themselves before tomorrow, for the LORD, the God of Israel, says: You are under the ban, O Israel. You cannot stand up to your enemies until you remove from among you whoever has incurred the ban. ¹⁴In the morning you must present yourselves by tribes. The tribe which the LORD designates shall come forward by clans; the clan which the LORD designates shall come forward by families; the family which the LORD designates shall come forward one by one. ¹⁵He who is designated as having incurred the ban shall be destroyed by fire, with all that is his, because he has violated the covenant of the LORD and has committed a shameful crime in Israel."

Achan's Guilt and Punishment ¹⁶Early the next morning Joshua had Israel come forward by tribes, and the tribe of Judah was designated. ¹⁷Then he had the clans of Judah come forward, and the clan of Zerah was designated. He had the clan of Zerah come forward by families, and Zabdi was designated. ¹⁸Finally he had that family come forward one by one, and Achan, son of Carmi, son of Zabdi, son of Zerah of the tribe of Judah, was designated. ¹⁹Joshua said to Achan, "My son, give to the LORD, the God of Israel, glory and honor by telling me what you have done; do not hide it from me. ²⁰Achan answered Joshua, "I have indeed sinned against the LORD, the God of Israel. This is what I have done: ²¹Among the spoils, I saw a beautiful Babylonian mantle, two hundred shekels of silver, and a bar of gold fifty shekels in weight; in my greed I took them. They are now hidden in the ground inside my tent, with the silver underneath." ²²The messengers whom Joshua sent hastened to the tent and found them hidden there, with the silver underneath. ²³They took them from the tent, brought them to Joshua and all the Israelites, and spread them out before the LORD.

²⁴Then Joshua and all Israel took Achan, son of Zerah, with the silver, the mantle, and the bar of gold, and with his

In the Lord's response (vv. 10-15) Joshua learns of the reason for the defeat, namely, that Israel has taken goods subject to the ban and so has violated the covenant. Israel is now under the ban and the Lord cannot and will not remain with Israel unless she removes from her midst the one who has incurred the ban. The legal procedure described (v. 14) is that of a trial by sacred lot, though we are given no details of the procedure. The verses express clearly the idea that the whole community can suffer for the sins of one.

Once Achan is identified as the culprit, he and all of his possessions are taken to the valley of Achor and stoned, and the Lord's anger toward Israel relents (vv. 16-26). The final verses present two etiologies as an explanation of the story of Achan. One of them explains a pile of stones in the valley

sons and daughters, his ox, his ass and his sheep, his tent, and all his possessions, and led them off to the Valley of Achor. ²⁵Joshua said, "The LORD bring upon you today the misery with which you have afflicted us!" And all Israel stoned him to death ²⁶and piled a great heap of stones over him, which remains to the present day. Then the anger of the LORD relented. That is why the place is called the Valley of Achor to this day.

8 **Capture of Ai.** ¹The LORD then said to Joshua, "Do not be afraid or dismayed. Take all the army with you and prepare to attack Ai. I have delivered the king of Ai into your power, with his people, city, and land. ²Do to Ai and its king what you did to Jericho and its king; except that you may take its spoil and livestock as booty. Set an ambush behind the city." ³So Joshua and all the soldiers prepared to attack Ai. Picking out thirty thousand warriors, Joshua sent them off by night ⁴with these orders: "See that you ambush the city from the rear, at no great distance; then all of you be on the watch.

⁵The rest of the people and I will come up to the city, and when they make a sortie against us as they did the last time, we will flee from them. ⁶They will keep coming out after us until we have drawn them away from the city, for they will think we are fleeing from them as we did the last time. When this occurs, ⁷rise from ambush and take possession of the city, which the LORD, your God, will deliver into your power. ⁸When you have taken the city, set it afire in obedience to the LORD's command. These are my orders to you." ⁹Then Joshua sent them away. They went to the place of ambush, taking up their position to the west of Ai, toward Bethel. Joshua, however, spent that night in the plain.

¹⁰Early the next morning Joshua mustered the army and went up to Ai at its head, with the elders of Israel. ¹¹When all the troops he led were drawn up in position before the city, they pitched camp north of Ai, on the other side of the ravine. ¹²[He took about five thousand men and set them in ambush between

of Achor (v. 26); the other, the name of the valley of Achor (vv. 24 and 26). This latter etiology is developed through a play on the words "Achor" and "Achan" and by the fact that the Hebrew root for "misery" and "afflicted" (see v. 25) is similar in sound to "Achor." More importantly, however, the purpose of the story is to explain to the exiles that the violation of the covenant leads to defeat.

Now that the Lord's anger against Israel has relented, the Lord tells Joshua to prepare to attack Ai. Notice that in contrast to chapter 7 victory is assured (8:1) because it is the Lord who leads Israel into battle. Hence, Israel is not to be afraid; she is only to be obedient and destroy Ai as she destroyed Jericho (v. 2). However, the Israelites are now allowed to take booty, and the Lord sets out the general lines of the conquest—it is to be through an ambush.

Joshua then gives instructions to the warriors who are to carry out the ambush (vv. 3-8), and they leave to take up their positions (v. 9). Notice again the emphasis that the Israelites will be able to take the city because the Lord has delivered it into their power (see 8:1).

Verses 10-23 describe the battle. As the main body of Israelites fled once again in seeming defeat before the king of Ai, all of the soldiers in Ai came

Bethel and Ai, west of the city.] ¹³Thus the people took up their stations, with the main body north of the city and the ambush west of it, and Joshua waited overnight among his troops. ¹⁴The king of Ai saw this, and he and all his army came out very early in the morning to engage Israel in battle at the descent toward the Arabah, not knowing that there was an ambush behind the city. ¹⁵Joshua and the main body of the Israelites fled in seeming defeat toward the desert, ¹⁶till the last of the soldiers in the city had been called out to pursue them. ¹⁷Since they were drawn away from the city, with every man engaged in this pursuit of Joshua and the Israelites, not a soldier remained in Ai [or Bethel], and the city was open and unprotected.

¹⁸Then the LORD directed Joshua, "Stretch out the javelin in your hand toward Ai, for I will deliver it into your power." Joshua stretched out the javelin in his hand toward to city, ¹⁹and as soon as he did so, the men in ambush rose from their post, rushed in, captured the city, and immediately set it on fire. ²⁰By the

time the men of Ai looked back, the smoke from the city was already skyhigh. Escape in any direction was impossible, because the Israelites retreating toward the desert now turned on their pursuers; ²¹for when Joshua and the main body of Israelites saw that the city had been taken from ambush and was going up in smoke, they struck back at the men of Ai. ²²Since those in the city came out to intercept them, the men of Ai were hemmed in by Israelites on either side, who cut them down without any fugitives or survivors ²³except the king, whom they took alive and brought to Joshua.

²⁴All the inhabitants of Ai who had pursued the Israelites into the desert were slain by the sword there in the open, down to the last man. Then all Israel returned and put to the sword those inside the city. ²⁵There fell that day a total of twelve thousand men and women, the entire population of Ai. ²⁶Joshua kept the javelin in his hand stretched out until he had fulfilled the doom on all the inhabitants of Ai. ²⁷However, the Israelites took for themselves as booty the livestock

out after the Israelites, leaving the city open and unprotected. When Joshua, at the Lord's command, stretches out his javelin towards Ai, the soldiers in ambush rise up and take the city, setting it on fire. By the time the soldiers of Ai realize what is happening, it is too late. They find themselves caught between the two parts of the Israelite army and are cut down to the last person. Only the king of Ai is spared, and he is taken alive and brought to Joshua. Joshua's stretching out of the javelin (v. 18 and v. 26) recalls the action of Moses during the war with Amalek (see Exod 17:8-13). This appears to be another incident in which the life of Joshua is paralleled to the life of Moses.

The story concludes (vv. 24-29) with the report of the slaying of all of the inhabitants of Ai (see Deut 20:16-18), the taking of booty, and the destruction of the city. These final verses contain another double etiology that explains how all was reduced to a mound of ruins, "as it remains today" (an explanation of the name of the city, "the ruin"), and how the pile of stones at the entrance of the city gate came into being—they were used to cover the body of the slain king of Ai.

and the spoil of that city, according to the command of the LORD issued to Joshua. ²⁸Then Joshua destroyed the place by fire, reducing it to an everlasting mound of ruins, as it remains today. ²⁹He had the king of Ai hanged on a tree until evening; then at sunset Joshua ordered the body removed from the tree and cast at the entrance of the city gate, where a great heap of stones was piled up over it, which remains to the present day.

Altar on Mount Ebal. ³⁰Later Joshua built an altar to the LORD, the God of Israel, on Mount Ebal, ³¹of unhewn stones on which no iron tool had been used, in keeping with the command to the Israelites of Moses, the servant of the LORD, as recorded in the book of the law. On this altar they offered holocausts and peace offerings to the LORD. ³²There, in the presence of the Israelites, Joshua inscribed upon the stones a copy of the law written by Moses. ³³And all Israel, stranger and native alike, with their elders, officers and judges, stood on either side of the ark facing the levitical priests who were carrying the ark of the covenant of the LORD. Half of them were facing Mount Gerizim and half Mount Ebal, thus carrying out the instructions of Moses, the servant of the LORD, for the blessing of the people of Israel on this first occasion. ³⁴Then were read aloud all the words of the law, the blessings and the curses, exactly as written in the book of the law. ³⁵Every single word that Moses had commanded, Joshua read aloud to the entire community, including the women and children, and the strangers who had accompanied Israel.

9 **Confederacy against Israel.** ¹When the news reached the kings west of the Jordan, in the mountain regions and in the foothills, and all along the coast of the

In contrast to chapter 7, chapter 8 shows how Israel, when she fights under the leadership of the Lord and does the Lord's will, can be victorious. The message for the exiles is clear: while sin leads to disaster, obedience leads to victory.

8:30-35 The altar on Mount Ebal. These verses are an editorial addition, since they interrupt the flow of the story in 8:29 and 9:1. The verses report the fulfillment of the commands of Moses (see Deut 27:1-8, 11-13 and Deut 11:29) concerning what is to happen once the people have entered the land. Notice the often repeated reference to Moses in these verses. We shall see later that these verses are closely related to the material in chapter 24.

Mounts Ebal and Gerizim face one another across a deep ravine in north central Israel, about 20 miles north of Ai. Between them is the city of Shechem, an ancient cultic site. These two mountains flanked the important east-west pass through the central hill country of Israel.

9:1-27 The Gibeonite alliance. The two narratives in verses 1-2 and 3-27 show the possible responses of a people threatened with total destruction: to form a common alliance against the threat, or to enter into an alliance with the threatening party.

The reference (v. 1) to the mountain region, the foothills, and the coast of the Great Sea identifies the three regions (from east to west) of the land of Palestine.

Great Sea as far as Lebanon: Hittites, Amorites, Canaanites, Perizzites, Hivites and Jebusites, ²they all formed an alliance to launch a common attack against Joshua and Israel.

The Gibeonite Deception. ³On learning what Joshua had done to Jericho and Ai, the inhabitants of Gibeon ⁴put into effect a device of their own. They chose provisions for a journey, making use of old sacks for their asses, and old wineskins, torn and mended. ⁵They wore old, patched sandals and shabby garments; and all the bread they took was dry and crumbly. ⁶Thus they journeyed to Joshua in the camp at Gilgal, where they said to him and to the men of Israel, "We have come from a distant land to propose that you make an alliance with us." But the men of Israel replied to the Hivites, "You may be living in land that is ours. How, then, can we make an alliance with you?" ⁸But they answered Joshua, "We are your servants." Then Joshua asked them, "Who are you? Where do you come from?" ⁹They answered him, "Your servants have come from a far-off land, because of the fame of the Lord, your God. For we have heard reports of all that he did in Egypt ¹⁰and all that he did to the two kings of the Amorites beyond the Jordan, Sihon, king of Heshbon, and Og, king of Bashan, who lived in Ashtaroth. ¹¹So our elders and all the inhabitants of our country said to us, 'Take along provisions for the journey and go to meet them. Say to them: We are your servants; we proposed that you make an alliance with us.' ¹²This bread of ours was still warm when we brought it from home as provisions the day we left to come to you, but now it is dry and crumbled. ¹³Here are our wineskins, which were new when we filled them, but now they are torn. Look at our garments and sandals, which are worn out from the very long journey." ¹⁴Then the Israelite princes partook of their provisions, without seeking the advice of the Lord. ¹⁵So Joshua made an alliance with them and entered into an agreement to spare them, which the princes of the community sealed with an oath.

The narrative about the Gibeonites in verses 3-27 reflects a complex literary history. Aside from D's later additions in verses 9-10, 24-25 and 27b, the figure of Joshua appears to have been a secondary insertion into the text, and verses 16-27 appear to be a secondary addition to the original story (one can jump from 9:15 to 10:1 without any sense of a gap). It is also not clear whether one city or four cities (see v. 17) entered into the alliance with Israel; nor is it always clear who was acting for Israel—the "men of Israel" or Joshua.

Like the story of Rahab (see ch. 2) this story is an etiology that has been preserved to explain the presence of the Gibeonites in the midst of Israel, despite the prohibitions of Deut 20:10-18, and their role as slaves (hewers of wood and drawers of water) at an Israelite sanctuary. The story also explains how Israel came into control of the central hill country and serves as background for chapter 10. For the exiles in the sixth century, the purpose of the story would have been to call them to faith in the power and promises of Yahweh (see vv. 9-10 and 24-25). There is little question about the historicity of an alliance between Israel and the Gibeonites (see 2 Sam 21:1-9).

Gibeonites Made Vassals. [16]Three days after the agreement was entered into, the Israelites learned that these people were from nearby, and would be living in Israel. [17]The third day on the road, the Israelites came to their cities of Gibeon, Chephirah, Beeroth and Kiriath-jearim, [18]but did not attack them, because the princes of the community had sworn to them by the LORD, the God of Israel. When the entire community grumbled against the princes, [19]these all remonstrated with the people, "We have sworn to them by the LORD, the God of Israel, and so we cannot harm them. [20]Let us therefore spare their lives and so deal with them that we shall not be punished for the oath we have sworn to them." [21]Thus the princes recommended that they be let live, as hewers of wood and drawers of water for the entire community; and the community did as the princes advised them.

[22]Joshua summoned the Gibeonites and said to them, "Why did you lie to us and say that you lived at a great distance from us, when you will be living in our very midst? [23]For this are you accursed: every one of you shall always be a slave [hewers of wood and drawers of water] for the house of my God." [24]They answered Joshua, "Your servants were fully informed of how the LORD, your God, commanded his servant Moses that you be given the entire land and that all its inhabitants be destroyed before you. Since, therefore, at your advance, we were in great fear for our lives, we acted as we did. [25]And now that we are in your power, do with us what you think fit and right." [26]Joshua did what he had decided:

The first part of the narrative (vv. 3-15) reports the deception of the Gibeonites and the conclusion of the alliance. Gibeon is identified with modern el-Jib, a site in the central hill country about seven miles northwest of Jerusalem and situated along an important east-west road from Jericho to the coastal plain. Seemingly, Gibeon belonged to a small four-village alliance (see v. 17). Whatever settlement existed at el-Jib in the time of Joshua, archaeological evidence shows that it was not a large settlement, although it later became an important city.

The Gibeonites come to Israel at Gilgal (v. 6), to which Israel has returned after the covenant ceremony reported in the preceding chapter. Israel's hesitancy regarding the proposed alliance (v. 7) flows from Deut 7:2 and 20:10-18. The alliance would have included peace between the two parties, as well as mutual defense (see 10:1-15). The reason given for seeking this alliance is the fame of the Lord, the God of Israel, and all that this God had done for Israel in Egypt and against Kings Sihon and Og (see Num 21:21-35). Israel, without seeking the advice of the Lord, agrees to the alliance and the parties partake of a covenant meal to seal it (vv. 14-15).

The second part of the narrative (vv. 16-27) reports the discovery of the ruse and Israel's response. The oath was so important that even the discovery of the trickery was not sufficient reason to release Israel from her obligations. However, the Gibeonites must be punished, so it is recommended that they be made "hewers of wood and drawers of water" (vv. 16-21), an expression referring to an inferior form of membership in the community (see

while he saved them from being killed by the Israelites, ²⁷at the same time he made them, as they still are, hewers of wood and drawers of water for the community and for the altar of the LORD, in the place of the LORD's choice.

10 **The Siege of Gibeon.** ¹Now Adonizedek, king of Jerusalem, heard that, in the capture and destruction of Ai, Joshua had done to that city and its king as he had done to Jericho and its king. He heard also that the inhabitants of Gibeon had made their peace with Israel, remaining among them, ²and that there was great fear abroad, because Gibeon was large enough for a royal city, larger even than the city of Ai, and all its men were brave. ³So Adonizedek, king of Jerusalem, sent for Hoham, king of Hebron, Piram, king of Jarmuth, Japhia,

king of Lachish, and Debir, king of Eglon, ⁴to come to his aid for an attack on Gibeon, since it had concluded peace with Joshua and the Israelites. ⁵The five Amorite kings, of Jerusalem, Hebron, Jarmuth, Lachish and Eglon, united all their forces and marched against Gibeon, where they took up siege positions. ⁶Thereupon, the men of Gibeon sent an appeal to Joshua in his camp at Gilgal: "Do not abandon your servants. Come up here quickly and save us. Help us, because all the Amorite kings of the mountain country have joined forces against us."

Joshua's Victory. ⁷So Joshua marched up from Gilgal with his picked troops and the rest of his soldiers. ⁸Meanwhile the LORD said to Joshua, "Do not fear them, for I have delivered them into your

Deut 29:10). Joshua confronts the Gibeonites and tells them that they are to carry out their tasks for "the house of my God" (v. 23). It is not clear if the reference here is to Gibeon or Gilgal. In their response (vv. 24-25) the Gibeonites seem to reflect a knowledge of Deut 20:10-18.

10:1-43 The conquest of the south. In a series of related incidents Joshua takes control of the southern part of Israel. The occasion for this conquest is the attack on Gibeon by the five kings from the south.

10:1-27 The Gibeon campaign. When Adonizedek, the king of Jerusalem, hears of how Joshua has dealt with Ai and Jericho and their kings, and that Gibeon has made a covenant with Israel, he becomes frightened and sends for four other kings from the neighborhood to help him attack Gibeon (vv. 1-4). The fear springs from the strength of Gibeon and because Gibeon has gone over to Israel, thus giving Israel an important bridgehead in the central hill country. Thus, the five kings put Gibeon under siege, as a way of stopping Israel's advance into the hill country, and as a punishment. The Gibeon in chapter 10, "large enough for a royal city" (v. 2), contrasts with the Gibeon in chapter 9, so weak that it sought an alliance with Israel. The picture presented in chapter 10 is also at odds with archaeological evidence. When the Gibeonites appeal to their protector, Joshua, he responds immediately and, after an all-night march, takes the five kings by surprise and inflicts a great slaughter on them (vv. 5-10). The march would have covered about eighteen miles along mountainous roads. Note that Joshua is victorious because the Lord has delivered the five kings into his power (v. 8). The

power. Not one of them will be able to withstand you." ⁹And when Joshua made his surprise attack upon them after an all-night march from Gilgal, ¹⁰the LORD threw them into disorder before him. The Israelites inflicted a great slaughter on them at Gibeon and pursued them down the Beth-horon slope, harassing them as far as Azekah and Makkedah.

¹¹While they fled before Israel along the descent from Beth-horon, the LORD hurled great stones from the sky above them all the way to Azekah, killing many. More died from these hailstones than the Israelites slew with the sword. ¹²On this day, when the LORD delivered up the Amorites to the Israelites,
Joshua prayed to the LORD,
and said in the presence of Israel:
Stand still, O sun, at Gibeon,
O moon, in the valley of Aijalon!
¹³And the sun stood still,
and the moon stayed,
while the nation took vengeance
on its foes.

Is this not recorded in the Book of Jashar? The sun halted in the middle of the sky; not for a whole day did it resume its swift course. ¹⁴Never before or since was there a day like this, when the LORD obeyed the voice of a man; for the LORD fought for Israel. ¹⁵[Then Joshua and all Israel returned to the camp at Gilgal.]

Execution of Amorite Kings. ¹⁶Meanwhile the five kings who had fled, hid in a cave at Makkedah. ¹⁷When Joshua was told that the five kings had been discovered hiding in a cave at Makkedah, ¹⁸he said, "Roll large stones to the mouth of the cave and post men over it to guard them. ¹⁹But do not remain there yourselves. Pursue your enemies, and harry them in the rear. Do not allow them to escape to their cities, for the LORD, your God, has delivered them into your power."

²⁰Once Joshua and the Israelites had finally inflicted the last blows in this very great slaughter, and the survivors had escaped from them into the fortified cities,

hailstones mentioned in verse 11 were, no doubt, the result of an unusually severe midsummer storm that wreaked as much havoc as the army of Israel. Beth-horon was the name of an important pass that was a major point of entry from the west into the hill country.

Verses 12-14 should not be taken too literally. The compiler certainly understood them to be the description of a miraculous prolonging of the day so that Joshua would have enough sunlight to finish off the enemy. However, we should view these verses as a poetic description emphasizing that Yahweh fought for Israel and was responsible for the victory. Much of this story is reported in Judg 1:4-20, where three of the cities listed here are said to have been captured by the tribe of Judah.

Verses 16-27 describe the death of the five kings who had initiated the attack on Gibeon. Makkedah was west of Jerusalem. When the kings are discovered, Joshua does not want to waste time with them. He tells his men, after making sure that the kings cannot escape, to pursue the fleeing soldiers, and to kill them before they escape into their fortified cities (vv. 16-19). The later humiliation of the kings (v. 24) was meant to build up the confidence of Israel and to emphasize the power of the Lord in her midst. The story ends on an etiological note that explains the existence of a pile of stones at

²¹all the army returned safely to Joshua and the camp at Makkedah, no man uttering a sound against the Israelites. ²²Then Joshua said, "Open the mouth of the cave and bring out those five kings to me." ²³Obediently, they brought out to him from the cave the five kings, of Jerusalem, Hebron, Jarmuth, Lachish and Eglon. ²⁴When they had done so, Joshua summoned all the men of Israel and said to the commanders of the soldiers who had marched with him, "Come forward and put your feet on the necks of these kings." They came forward and put their feet upon their necks. ²⁵Then Joshua said to them, "Do not be afraid or dismayed, be firm and steadfast. This is what the LORD will do to all the enemies against whom you fight." ²⁶Thereupon Joshua struck and killed them, and hanged them on five trees, where they remained hanging until evening. ²⁷At sunset they were removed from the trees at the command of Joshua and cast into the cave where they had hidden; over the mouth of the cave large stones were placed, which remain until this very day.

Conquest of Southern Canaan. ²⁸Makkedah, too, Joshua captured and put to the sword at that time. He fulfilled the doom on the city, on its king, and on every person in it, leaving no survivors. Thus he did to the king of Makkedah what he had done to the king of Jericho. ²⁹Joshua then passed on with all Israel from Makkedah to Libnah, which he attacked. ³⁰Libnah also, with its king, the LORD delivered into the power of Israel. He put it to the sword with every person there, leaving no survivors. Thus he did to its king what he had done to the king of Jericho. ³¹Joshua next passed on with all Israel from Libnah to Lachish, where they set up a camp during the attack. ³²The LORD delivered Lachish into the power of Israel, so that on the second day Joshua captured it and put it to the sword with every person in it, just as he had done to Libnah. ³³At that time Horam, King of Gezer, came up to help Lachish, but Joshua defeated him and his people, leaving him no survivors. ³⁴From Lachish, Joshua passed on with all Israel to Eglon; encamping near it, they attacked it ³⁵and

the mouth of a cave in Makkedah (v. 27). The point of the story, then, is to build up the confidence of the exiles in the power of their God to overcome their enemies (see vv. 8-14 and 25).

10:28-43 The conquest of the south concluded. Having defeated the coalition of five kings, Joshua follows up this victory with raids against six cities to the west and southwest of Jerusalem (vv. 28-39). The descriptions of these raids follow a definite pattern that reports how the city was captured and its inhabitants put to the sword with no survivors. In this way Joshua fulfilled the doom on each city according to the will of the Lord (Deut 20:10-18). Israel was successful because the Lord had delivered the cities into her power.

It is not possible to harmonize fully the description of the coalition in verses 1-5 with the account of the campaign against the south depicted in these verses. While there is some overlapping of cities, verses 28-39 seem to reflect a tradition different from the one in verses 1-5. What seems to lie behind these verses is a presupposition that Israel's enemies always followed the same route when advancing against Jerusalem at different points in

captured it the same day, putting it to the sword. He fulfilled the doom that day on every person in it, just as he had done at Lachish. ³⁶From Eglon, Joshua went up with all Israel to Hebron, which they attacked ³⁷and captured. They put it to the sword with its king, all its towns, and every person there, leaving no survivors, just as Joshua had done to Eglon. He fulfilled the doom on it and on every person there. ³⁸Then Joshua and all Israel turned back to Debir and attacked it, ³⁹capturing it with its king and all its towns. They put them to the sword and fulfilled the doom on every person there, leaving no survivors. Thus was done to Debir and its king what had been done to Hebron, as well as to Libnah and its king.

⁴⁰Joshua conquered the entire country; the mountain regions, the Negeb, the foothills, and the mountain slopes, with all their kings. He left no survivors, but fulfilled the doom on all who lived there, just as the LORD, the God of Israel, had commanded. ⁴¹Joshua conquered from Kadesh-barnea to Gaza, and all the land of Goshen to Gibeon. ⁴²All these kings and their lands Joshua captured in a single campaign, for the LORD, the God of Israel, fought for Israel. ⁴³Thereupon Joshua with all Israel returned to the camp at Gilgal.

11 **Northern Confederacy.** ¹When Jabin, king of Hazor, learned of this, he sent a message to Jobab, king of Madon, to the king of Shimron, to the king of Achshaph, ²and to the northern

history. It was the route of Sennacherib in 701 B.C. (see 2 Kgs 18:13) and of Nebuchadnezzar in 587 B.C. (see Jer 34:7) when they advanced on Jerusalem.

The concluding verses (40-43) summarize this part of the conquest. The author's purpose is to show that Israel had conquered all of the territory south of Gibeon under Joshua's leadership. The description is highly exaggerated, the author using the summary to emphasize how Joshua had followed the Lord's commands and had been successful because the Lord fought for Israel. Again, the message for the exiles is clear: they are to be obedient and trust in the power of the Lord.

11:1-15 The conquest of the north. The chapter begins abruptly with no clear connection to the preceding material except that the king of Hazor "learned of this." Originally, this material was probably an independent tradition that is now presented as the northern counterpart to the conquest of the south reported in chapter 10. This tradition may have belonged to one or more northern tribes and was later extended to all Israel. So too, the figure of Joshua has probably been introduced into the story secondarily. However, the tradition seems to rest upon a historical foundation. Notice that this chapter follows the same outline as chapter 10: one king forms a coalition to defeat the Israelites, but Joshua defeats the coalition through a surprise move, and attacks the cities involved.

The narrative begins with Jabin, the king of Hazor, calling together a coalition of northern kings. Notice how the description begins with specific

kings in the mountain regions and the Arabah near Chinneroth, in the foothills, and in Naphath-dor to the west. ³These were Canaanites to the east and west, Amorites, Hittites, Perizzites and Jebusites in the mountain regions, and Hivites at the foot of Hermon in the land of Mizpah. ⁴They came out with all their troops, an army numerous as the sands on the seashore, and with a multitude of horses and chariots. ⁵All these kings joined forces and marched to the waters of Merom, where they encamped together to fight against Israel.

⁶The LORD said to Joshua, "Do not fear them, for by this time tomorrow I will stretch them slain before Israel. You must hamstring their horses and burn their chariots." ⁷Joshua with his whole army came upon them at the waters of Merom in a surprise attack. ⁸The LORD delivered them into the power of the Israelites, who defeated them and pursued them to Greater Sidon, to Misrephoth-maim, and eastward to the valley of Mizpeh. They struck them all down leaving no survivors. ⁹Joshua did to them as the LORD had commanded: he hamstrung their horses and burned their chariots.

Conquest of Northern Canaan. ¹⁰At that time Joshua, turning back, captured Hazor and slew its king with the sword; for Hazor formerly was the chief of all those kingdoms. ¹¹He also fulfilled the

details and then becomes more and more vague. All of the members of the coalition, with their troops, horses, and chariots, now gather together at the waters of Merom, a few miles southwest of Hazor, to launch an attack against Israel (vv. 1-5). The topography of these chapters covers the general area of Galilee, an area that was later assigned to the tribe of Naphtali. Archaeological excavations show that Hazor, located about eight miles north of the Sea of Galilee, was a very impressive city in the thirteenth century B.C. and could well have fit the descriptions of it in these verses. Excavations also show that it was destroyed in the mid-thirteenth century, which would coincide with the time of Joshua. The other three cities named here are located south of Hazor. The Arabah is the great rift that contains the Sea of Galilee (here called "Chinnereth"), the Jordan River, and the Dead Sea. The size of the opposing army is no doubt exaggerated here to magnify the victory.

Israel was successful against the coalition because the Lord had delivered the Canaanites into her power and because Joshua had obeyed the Lord by following the tactics laid out for him (vv. 6-9). Notice that nothing is said about where Joshua received the word of the Lord. From the context it would seem that he was still at Gilgal. The crippling of the horses prevented the Canaanites from using their chariots, which were subsequently burned. The Canaanites then had to flee on foot, allowing Israel to defeat them. Since Israel did not begin to use chariots until the time of David and Solomon, it is doubtful that they could have defeated a chariot-equipped army.

The reason for Joshua's actions against Hazor is that Hazor had been the chief of all those kingdoms (vv. 10-12). Behind the remark about Israel not burning any of the other cities "built on raised sites" (v. 13) is a reminder

doom by putting every person there to the sword, till none was left alive. Hazor itself he burned. ¹²Joshua thus captured all those kings with their cities and put them to the sword, fulfilling the doom on them, as Moses, the servant of the Lord, had commanded. ¹³However, Israel did not destroy by fire any of the cities built on raised sites, except Hazor, which Joshua burned. ¹⁴The Israelites took all the spoil and livestock of these cities as their booty; but the people they put to the sword, until they had exterminated the last of them, leaving none alive. ¹⁵As the Lord had commanded his servant Moses, so Moses commanded Joshua, and Joshua acted accordingly. He left nothing undone that the Lord had commanded Moses should be done.

Survey of the Conquest. ¹⁶So Joshua captured all this land: the mountain regions, the entire Negeb, all the land of Goshen, the foothills, the Arabah, as well as the mountain regions and foothills of Israel, ¹⁷from Mount Halak that rises toward Seir as far as Baal-gad in the Lebanon valley at the foot of Mount Hermon. All their kings he captured and put to death. ¹⁸Joshua waged war against all these kings for a long time. ¹⁹With the exception of the Hivites who lived in Gibeon, no city made peace with the Israelites; all were taken in battle. ²⁰For it was the design of the Lord to encourage

that Israel had neither the strength nor the technical knowledge to defeat the chariot armies of the Canaanites. The extent of the program of destruction described in these verses is, therefore, probably exaggerated.

This section concludes with a summary regarding the obedience of Joshua: he did all that the Lord had commanded Moses (v. 15). The message to the exiles is reiterated: the need for obedience to the Lord and trust in the power of the Lord. With such trust, victory is possible.

11:16–12:24 Summary of the conquest. The conquest is now summarized in an idealistic fashion by two separate texts. The editorial summary in 11:16-23 was the original summary and conclusion to the narrative. Chapter 12, with its list of conquered kings, was inserted later.

11:16-23 Editorial summary. These verses come from the original compiler of the conquest stories. The basic theme, set out in verses 16 and 23, is that Joshua "captured all this land." Therefore, the Lord has kept all the promises made to Moses (see Josh 1:1-9). The description of the conquered land (vv. 16-17) goes significantly beyond the description in the preceding chapters and also beyond the classical description of "from Dan to Beersheba." Mount Halak, which marks the southern boundary, is at the southern end of the Negeb desert, south of Judah. Baalgad, the northern boundary, refers to a site at the southern end of the Beka valley in Lebanon.

Verse 18 attempts to correct any notion that the conquest was swift. It is pointed out that Israel had to do battle with all these cities because it was the will of the Lord. The Lord had designed it so that all the cities, except Gibeon, would wage war against Israel and so give reason for their extermination (see Deut 20:10-20).

them to wage war against Israel, that they might be doomed to destruction and thus receive no mercy, but be exterminated, as the LORD had commanded Moses.

²¹At that time Joshua penetrated the mountain regions and exterminated the Anakim in Hebron, Debir, Anab, the entire mountain region of Judah, and the entire mountain region of Israel. Joshua fulfilled the doom on them and on their cities, ²²so that no Anakim were left in the land of the Israelites. However, some survived in Gaza, in Gath, and in Ashdod. ²³Thus Joshua captured the whole country, just as the LORD had foretold to Moses. Joshua gave it to Israel as their heritage, apportioning it among the tribes. And the land enjoyed peace.

12 Lists of Conquered Kings. ¹The kings of the land east of the Jordan, from the River Arnon to Mount Hermon, including all the eastern section of the Arabah, whom the Israelites conquered and whose land they occupied, were: ²First, Sihon, king of the Amorites, who lived in Heshbon. His domain extended from Aroer, which is on the bank of the Wadi Arnon, to include the wadi itself, and the land northward through half of Gilead to the Wadi Jabbok, ³as well as the Arabah from the eastern side of the Sea of Chinnereth, as far south as the eastern side of the Salt Sea of the Arabah in the direction of Bethjeshimoth, to a point under the slopes of Pisgah. ⁴Secondly, Og, king of Bashan, a survivor of the Rephaim, who lived at Ashtaroth and Edrei. ⁵He ruled over Mount Hermon, Salecah, and all Bashan as far as the boundary of the Geshurites

Verses 21-22 are a bit jarring in the context. The Anakim are described elsewhere as "giants" (Num 13:33). The editor wants to show that there were trouble spots where not all the indigenous population had been driven out.

Once more, the conclusion in verse 23 emphasizes that the Lord has kept the promises made to Moses. The same verse forms the transition to the apportioning of the land that begins in chapter 13. The insistence on the Lord's fidelity to the promises made to Moses was an important message for the people in exile.

12:1-24 List of conquered kings. This chapter falls into two parts: a listing of the kings conquered by the Israelites under Moses, east of the Jordan (vv. 1-6), and a listing of those kings whom Israel had conquered under Joshua, west of the Jordan (vv. 7-24). The chapter is an elaboration of 11:23, and is intended to emphasize that the whole country had been conquered by Israel.

The material in verses 1-6 has been developed from Deut 3:8-17 and Josh 13:9-32. Verse 1 points out the northern and southern boundaries of the territory conquered east of the Jordan, namely, Mount Hermon in the north and the River Arnon in the south. The southern half of this area from the River Arnon to the River Jabbok had belonged to Sihon, king of the Amorites, who had his capital in Heshbon (vv. 2-3). The area north of the Jabbok had been under the control of Og, king of Bashan (vv. 4-5). Num 21:21-35 (see Deut 2:26–3:11) recounts the defeat of Sihon and Og. Num 32 reports how Moses had assigned this land to the Reubenites, Gadites, and the half-tribe

and Maacathites, and over half of Gilead as far as the territory of Sihon, king of Heshbon. ⁶After Moses, the servant of the LORD and the Israelites conquered them, he assigned their land to the Reubenites, the Gadites, and the half-tribe of Manasseh, as their property. ⁷This is a list of the kings whom Joshua and the Israelites conquered west of the Jordan and whose land, from Baal-gad in the Lebanon valley to Mount Halak which rises toward Seir, Joshua apportioned to the tribes of Israel. ⁸It included the mountain regions and foothills, the Arabah, the slopes, the desert, and the Negeb, belonging to the Hittites, Amorites, Canaanites, Perizzites, Hivites and Jebusites. ⁹They were the kings of Jericho, Ai (which is near Bethel), ¹⁰Jerusalem, Hebron, ¹¹Jarmuth, Lachish, ¹²Eglon, Gezer, ¹³Debir, Geder, ¹⁴Hormah, Arad, ¹⁵Libnah, Adullam, ¹⁶Makkedah, Bethel, ¹⁷Tappuah, Hepher, ¹⁸Aphek, Lasharon, ¹⁹Madon, Hazor, ²⁰Shimron, Achshaph, ²¹Taanach, Megiddo, ²²Kedesh, Jokneam (at Carmel), ²³and Dor (in Naphath-dor), the foreign king at Gilgal, ²⁴and the king of Tirzah, thirty-one kings in all.

II: DIVISION OF THE LAND

13 Division of Land Commanded. ¹When Joshua was old and ad-

of Manasseh (v. 6). The Rephaim mentioned in verse 4 were a legendary people of great stature who had inhabited Syria and Palestine in ages past (see Deut 2:11, 3:11; Gen 14:5; 2 Sam 21:16-20).

The listing of the kings conquered west of the Jordan in verses 7-24 is a very important list because verses 13b-24 contain names of cities not previously mentioned. These latter verses are not simply a summary of the preceding stories but represent an independent tradition of the conquest that some scholars say is very ancient, dating from the time of Solomon. Verses 16b-24 are especially interesting, since they list cities found in the territories of Ephraim and Manasseh in central Palestine, where no previous conquests have been mentioned.

The impression given by these lists is that of a total conquest of the land; and that is almost certainly the intention of the author. The interest of the author in these chapters of the conquest (6-11) has not been to give an exact historical account, but rather to show God keeping past promises through great acts on behalf of Israel.

PART II: THE DIVISION OF THE LAND

Josh 13:1–22:34

13-22 The division of the land. These chapters contain elaborate geographical details about how the land was divided among the various tribes, and provide statistical information about persons, places, and tribes. Their purpose is to show how God has given the whole country to Israel as its

vanced in years, the LORD said to him: "Though now you are old and advanced in years, a very large part of the land still remains to be conquered. ²This additional land includes all Geshur and all the districts of the Philistines ³(from the stream adjoining Egypt to the boundary of Ekron in the north is reckoned Canaanite territory, through held by the five lords of the Philistines in Gaza, Ashdod, Ashkelon, Gath and Ekron); also where the Avvim are in the south; ⁴all the land of the Canaanites from Mearah of the Sidonians to Aphek, and the boundaries of the Amorites; ⁵and the Gebalite territory; and all the Lebanon on the east, from Baal-gad at the foot of Mount Hermon to Labo in the land of Hamath. ⁶At the advance of the Israelites I will drive out all the Sidonian inhabitants of the

heritage, just as the Lord had promised Moses (see 11:23). This was an important message for the original audience of this book, the exiles, who had recently lost the land. To these exiles the Book of Joshua is promising above all that the Lord is faithful to the ancient promises made to the patriarchs.

The data found in these chapters are the result of combining various sources. Martin Noth claims that the section is the result of combining two documents: a list of towns of the kingdom of Judah, which dates from the time of King Josiah (d. 621), and a survey of boundaries dating from before the monarchy. Admittedly, the roots of some of this data are quite old, but the chapters reflect the impact of later events. This section may have been composed before the writing of Joshua, and may even be a later insertion into the original narrative of the conquest (compare 13:1b and 23:1b).

While the primary interest of these chapters is with the area west of the Jordan, the section begins with a survey of the allotments of the land east of the Jordan that Moses had made to the tribes of Reuben, Gad, and the half-tribe of Manasseh (13:8-33). It concludes with the narrative of the return of these tribes to their territory in order to take possession of it (ch. 22). Chapters 14-21 deal with the allotment to Judah and the Joseph tribes at Gilgal (14-17), the allotment at Shiloh to the remaining seven tribes (18-19), and the setting aside of the cities of asylum (20) and the Levitical cities (21).

In the material that follows, this commentary will not present a detailed analysis of the boundaries and lists of towns given in the biblical text. Readers interested in such detail are referred to the more technical commentaries and atlases. This commentary will limit itself to general remarks.

13:1-33 Introduction to the division of the land. With Joshua far advanced in years, the Lord orders him to apportion the land west of the Jordan among the nine tribes and the half-tribe of Manasseh that still do not have land. This chapter is a D composition in which the author points out that not all of the territory to be allotted had been conquered (v. 1), describes the lands that must still be conquered (vv. 2-6), reminds the reader that the tribes of Reuben, Gad, and the half-tribe of Manasseh had already been

mountain regions between Lebanon and Misrephoth-maim; at least include these areas in the division of the Israelite heritage, just as I have commanded you. ⁷Now, therefore, apportion among the nine tribes and the half-tribe of Manasseh the land which is to be their heritage."

The Eastern Tribes. ⁸Now the other half of the tribe of Manasseh, as well as the Reubenites and Gadites, had received their heritage which Moses, the servant of the Lord, had given them east of the Jordan: ⁹from Aroer on the bank of the Wadi Arnon and the city in the wadi itself, through the tableland of Medeba and Dibon, ¹⁰with the rest of the cities of Sihon, king of the Amorites, who reigned in Heshbon, to the boundary of the Ammonites; ¹¹also Gilead and the territory of the Geshurites and Maacathites, all Mount Hermon, and all Bashan as far as Salecah, ¹²the entire kingdom in Bashan of Og, a survivor of the Rephaim, who reigned at Ashtaroth and Edrei. Though Moses conquered and occupied these territories, ¹³the Israelites did not dislodge the Geshurites and Maacathites, so that Geshur and Maacath survive in the midst of Israel to this day. ¹⁴However, to the tribe of Levi Moses assigned no heritage since, as the Lord had promised them, the Lord, the God of Israel, is their heritage.

Reuben. ¹⁵What Moses gave to the Reubenite clans: ¹⁶Their territory reached from Aroer, on the bank of the Wadi Arnon, and the city in the wadi itself, through the tableland about Medeba, ¹⁷to include Heshbon and all its towns which are on the tableland, Dibon, Bamoth-baal, Beth-baal-meon, ¹⁸Jahaz, Kedemoth, Mephaath, ¹⁹Kiriathaim, Sibmah, Zereth-shahar on the knoll within the valley, ²⁰Beth-peor, the slopes of Pisgah, Beth-jeshimoth, ²¹and the other cities of the tableland and, generally, of the kingdom of Sihon. This Amorite king, who reigned in Heshbon, Moses had killed, with his vassals, the princes of Midian, who were settled in the land: Evi, Rekem, Zur, Hur, and Reba; ²²and

allotted territory east of the Jordan by Moses (v. 8), and gives a general (vv. 9-13) and a specific description (vv. 15-31) of this land. Two footnotes have been added to explain why the tribe of Levi had not received an allotment of a block of territory like all the other tribes (v. 14 and v. 33). While the author's purpose seems clear, a certain lack of logic and continuity in these verses is apparent (compare v. 7 to vv. 1-6 and v. 14 to vv. 8-13). This tells us that there are several layers of material in these chapters.

Verses 1-7 identify the parts of Canaan that Israel had not been able to conquer. That verses 2-6 were added secondarily is apparent from the lack of connection between the description of the land to be conquered and the subsequent order to apportion the land among the nine and a half tribes (v. 7). The area envisioned by verses 2-6 is the area belonging to the empire of David and Solomon.

Verses 8-14 are another addition to the text to explain why Joshua was to apportion land only to nine and a half tribes (v. 8), and to give a general picture of this territory (vv. 9-13). These verses seem to be based on Deut 3.

Verses 15-31 describe the lands allotted to the tribes of Reuben and Gad and the half-tribe of Manasseh. The Reubenites receive the tableland stretch-

among their slain followers the Israelites put to the sword also the soothsayer Balaam, son of Beor. ²³The boundary of the Reubenites was the bank of the Jordan. These cities and their villages were the heritage of the clans of the Reubenites.

Gad. ²⁴What Moses gave to the Gadite clans: ²⁵Their territory included Jazer, all the cities of Gilead, and half the land of the Ammonites as far as Aroer, toward Rabbah ²⁶(that is, from Heshbon to Ramath-mizpeh and Betonim, and from Mahanaim to the boundary of Lodebar); ²⁷and in the Jordan valley: Beth-haram, Beth-nimrah, Succoth, Zaphon, the other part of the kingdom of Sihon, king of Heshbon, with the bank of the Jordan to the southeastern tip of the Sea of Chinnereth. ²⁸These cities and their villages were the heritage of the clans of the Gadites.

Manasseh. ²⁹What Moses gave to the clans of the half-tribe of Manasseh:

³⁰Their territory included Mahanaim, all of Bashan, the entire kingdom of Og, king of Bashan, and all the villages of Jair, which are sixty cities in Bashan. ³¹Half of Gilead, with Ashtaroth and Edrei, once the royal cities of Og in Bashan, fell to the descendants of Machir, son of Manasseh, for half the clans descended from Machir.

³²These are the portions which Moses gave when he was in the plains of Moab, beyond the Jordan east of Jericho. ³³However, Moses gave no heritage to the tribe of Levi, since the LORD himself, the God of Israel, is their heritage, as he promised.

14 **The Western Tribe.** ¹Here follow the portions which the Israelites received in the land of Canaan. Eleazar the priest, Joshua, son of Nun, and the heads of families in the tribes of the Israelites determined ²their heritage by lot, in accordance with the instructions

ing north of the Arnon River to Medeba and Heshbon; the Gadites receive the highlands north of Heshbon; and the half-tribe of Manasseh receives the area of Bashan and a portion of Gilead.

The chapter concludes with another reminder that Moses had apportioned these lands to these tribes when he was in the plains of Moab (v. 32).

14:1–21:42 Allotment of the land west of the Jordan. This is the core section of the second half of the Book of Joshua and falls into five sections: an introduction (14:1-5); the allotment to Judah and Joseph at Gilgal (14:6–17:18); the allotment at Shiloh to the remaining seven tribes (18:1–19:51); a list of the cities of asylum (20:1-9); and a listing of the Levitical cities (21:1-42).

14:1-5 Introduction. These verses present the specific introduction to the allotment of the land west of the Jordan. They stress that Eleazar the priest and Joshua and the heads of the families divided the land (v. 1), and that it was done by lot, in accordance with the instructions that the Lord had given through Moses (vv. 2 and 5; see Num 33:54; 34:13). It is also explained why the land was divided among twelve tribes, even though the tribe of Levi was not given a block of land, namely, because the descendants of Joseph formed two tribes (vv. 3-4).

In the later traditions in the Old Testament Eleazar the priest (v. 1) is presented as a son of Aaron (Exod 6:25; Lev 10:5; Num 3:2). Though the

the Lord had given through Moses concerning the remaining nine and a half tribes. ³For to two and a half tribes Moses had already given a heritage beyond the Jordan; and though the Levites were given no heritage among the tribes, ⁴the descendants of Joseph formed two tribes, Manasseh and Ephraim. The Levites themselves received no share of the land except cities to live in, with their pasture lands for the cattle and flocks.

⁵Thus, in apportioning the land, did the Israelites carry out the instructions of the Lord to Moses.

Caleb's Portion. ⁶When the Judahites came up to Joshua in Gilgal, the Kenizzite Caleb, son of Jephunneh, said to him: "You know what the Lord said to the man of God, Moses, about you and me in Kadesh-barnea. ⁷I was forty years old when the servant of the Lord, Moses, sent me from Kadesh-barnea to reconnoiter the land; and I brought back to him a conscientious report. ⁸My fellow scouts who went up with me discouraged the people, but I was completely loyal to the Lord, my God. ⁹On that occasion Moses swore this oath, 'The land where you have set foot shall become your heritage and that of your descendants forever, because you have been completely loyal to the Lord, my God.' ¹⁰Now, as he promised, the Lord has preserved me while Israel was journeying through the desert, for the forty-five years since the Lord spoke thus to Moses; and although I am now eighty-five years old, ¹¹I am still as strong today as I was the day Moses sent me forth, with no less vigor whether for war or for ordinary tasks. ¹²Give me, therefore, this mountain region which the Lord promised me that day, as you yourself heard. True, the Anakim are there with large fortified cities, but if the Lord is with me I shall be able to drive them out, as the Lord promised." ¹³Joshua blessed Caleb, son of Jephunneh, and gave him Hebron as his heritage. ¹⁴Therefore Hebron remains the heritage of the Kenizzite Caleb, son of Jephunneh, to the present day, because he was completely loyal to the Lord, the God of Israel. ¹⁵Hebron was formerly called Kiriath-arba, for Arba, the greatest among the Anakim. And the land enjoyed peace.

15 Boundaries of Judah. ¹The lot for the clans of the Judahite tribe fell

use of the lot is referred to several times in the Old Testament it is not clear from the contexts what was involved. The reason for the need to explain why Joseph's descendants formed two tribes (vv. 3-4) flows from the tradition that Israel was composed of twelve tribes. Not all of the traditions agreed, however, on the identity of the twelve tribes; and some traditions did not even recognize the twelve tribe schema. For example, while one tradition spoke of Joseph as one tribe (17:14-18), another tradition spoke of Joseph's descendants as two tribes. Hence, the editor clarifies from the beginning that the descendants of Joseph formed two tribes: Ephraim and Manasseh.

14:6–15:63 Allotment to the tribe of Judah. This section is composed of four units: the portion given to Caleb (14:6-15); the list of the boundaries of Judah (15:1-12); the gift to Othniel (15:13-19); and the list of the cities of Judah (15:20-63).

14:6-15 Caleb's portion. The story tells how Caleb came into possession of the city of Hebron: it was a reward for his loyalty to the Lord when

in the extreme south toward the boundary of Edom, the desert of Zin in the Negeb. ²The boundary there ran from the bay that forms the southern end of the Salt Sea, ³southward below the pass of Akrabbim, across through Zin, up to a point south of Kadesh-barnea, across to Hezron, and up to Addar; from there, looping around Karka, ⁴it crossed to Azmon and then joined the Wadi of Egypt before coming out at the sea. [This is your southern boundary.] ⁵The eastern boundary was the Salt Sea as far as the mouth of the Jordan.

⁶The northern boundary climbed from the bay where the Jordan meets the sea, up to Beth-hoglah, and ran north of Betharabah, up to Eben-Bohan-ben-Reuben. ⁷Thence it climbed to Debir, north of the vale of Achor, in the direction of the Gilgal that faces the pass of Adummim,

on the south side of the wadi; from there it crossed to the waters of En-shemesh and emerged at En-rogel. ⁸Climbing again to the Valley of Ben-Hinnom on the southern flank of the Jebusites [that is, Jerusalem], the boundary rose to the top of the mountain at the northern end of the Valley of Hinnom on the west. ⁹From the top of the mountain it ran to the fountain of waters of Nephtoah, extended to the cities of Mount Ephron, and continued to Baalah, or Kiriath-jearim. ¹⁰From Baalah the boundary curved westward to Mount Seir and passed north of the ridge of Mount Jearim (that is, Chesalon); thence it descended to Bethshemesh, and ran across to Timnah. ¹¹It then extended along the northern flank of Ekron, continued through Shikkeron, and across to Mount Baalah, thence to include Jabneel, before it came out at the sea.

Moses had sent him to spy out the land many years earlier. Num 13–14 (see Deut 1:20-45) reports how all the spies, except Caleb and Joshua, advised against invasion. As a result God delayed the conquest until that whole generation, except Caleb and Joshua, had died. While a specific promise of land to Caleb is not found in Num 13–14, it is presupposed in Deut 1:36.

In several Old Testament passages, Caleb is identified as a Judahite (e.g., Num 13:6; 34:19), but elsewhere as a Kenizzite (e.g., Num 32:12). The Kenizzites were originally part of the Edomite people (Gen 36:11, 15, 42) who had settled in the southern hill country of Judah and were eventually assimilated into the tribe of Judah. Accordingly, Caleb is presumed to be part of the tribe of Judah. Note that in Judg 1:10 the region shown here as occupied by Caleb was conquered by Judah and Simeon, who defeated the three Anakim chiefs.

Because this passage, as well as 15:13-19, disrupts an otherwise carefully organized presentation of tribal allotments, some claim that they were inserted into the text secondarily. Some also argue that 14:6-15 originally followed 11:21-23 and that 15:13-19 has been drawn from Judg 1:10-20.

15:1-12 Boundaries of Judah. This first of the boundary lists is also the most detailed, indicating that the D editor had more complete records for Judah than for the other tribes. The list, though idealistic, is ancient, and may predate the period of the monarchy. It is certainly older than the list of cities in 15:21-62.

¹²The western boundary was the Great Sea and its coast. This was the complete boundary of the clans of the Judahites. **Conquest by Caleb.** ¹³As the LORD had commanded, Joshua gave Caleb, son of Jephunneh, a portion among the Judahites, namely, Kiriath-arba (Arba was the father of Anak), that is, Hebron. ¹⁴And Caleb drove out from there the three Anakim, the descendants of Anak: Sheshai, Ahiman and Talmai. ¹⁵From there he marched up against the inhabitants of Debir, which was formerly called Kiriath-sepher. ¹⁶Caleb said, "I will give my daughter Achsah in marriage to the one who attacks Kiriath-sepher and captures it." ¹⁷Othniel, son of Caleb's brother Kenaz, captured it, and so Caleb gave him his daughter Achsah in marriage. ¹⁸On the day of her marriage to Othniel, she induced him to ask her father for some land. Then, as she alighted from the ass, Caleb asked her, "What is troubling you?" ¹⁹She answered, "Give me an additional gift! Since you have assigned to me land in the Negeb, give me also pools of water." So he gave her the upper and lower pools.

Cities of Judah. ²⁰This is the heritage of the clans of the tribe of Judahites: ²¹The cities of the tribe of the Judahites in the extreme southern district toward Edom were: Kabzeel, Eder, Jagur, ²²Kinah, Dimonah, Adadah, ²³Kedesh, Hazor and Ithnan; ²⁴Ziph, Telem, Bealoth, ²⁵Hazor-hadattah, and Kerioth-hezron (that is,

Hazor); ²⁶Amam, Shema, Moladah, ²⁷Hazar-gaddah, Heshmon, Beth-pelet, ²⁸Hazar-shual, Beer-sheba, and Biziothiah, ²⁹Baalah, Iim, Ezem, ³⁰Eltolad, Chesil, Hormah, ³¹Ziklag, Madmannah, Sansannah, ³²Lebaoth, Shilhim and En-rimmon; a total of twenty-nine cities with their villages.

³³In the foothills: Eshtaol, Zorah, Ashnah, ³⁴Zanoah, Engannim, Tappuah, Enam, ³⁵Jarmuth, Adullam, Socoh, Azekah, ³⁶Shaaraim, Adithaim, Gederah, and Gederothaim; fourteen cities and their villages. ³⁷Zenan, Hadashah, Migdal-gad, ³⁸Dilean, Mizpeh, Joktheel, ³⁹Lachish, Bozkath, Eglon, ⁴⁰Cabbon, Lahmam, Chitlish, ⁴¹Gederoth, Beth-dagon, Naamah and Makkedah; sixteen cities and their villages. ⁴²Libnah, Ether, Ashan, ⁴³Iphtah, Ashnah, Nezib, ⁴⁴Keilah, Achzib and Mareshah; nine cities and their villages. ⁴⁵Ekron and its towns and villages; ⁴⁶from Ekron to the sea, all the towns that lie alongside Ashdod and their villages; ⁴⁷Ashdod and its towns and villages; Gaza and its towns and villages, as far as the Wadi of Egypt and the coast of the Great Sea.

⁴⁸In the mountain regions: Shamir, Jattir, Socoh, ⁴⁹Dannah, Kiriath-sannah (that is, Debir), ⁵⁰Anab, Eshtemoh, Anim, ⁵¹Goshen, Holon and Giloh; eleven cities and their villages. ⁵²Arab, Dumah, Eshan, ⁵³Janim, Beth-tappuah, Aphekah, ⁵⁴Humtah, Kiriath-arba (that is Hebron), and Zior; nine cities and their villages.

15:13-19 The gift to Othniel. This story, an almost verbatim duplicate of Judg 1:10-15, is an etiology to explain why the Othnielites, who also belonged to the Kenizzite group, had access to pools of water which should have belonged to the Calebites in Hebron. Notice that Caleb is said here to have taken by force the area given him as his heritage in 14:6-15.

15:20-63 Cities of Judah. This list of cities is based on a catalog of twelve provinces that composed the southern kingdom of Judah, probably drawn up for governmental administrative purposes sometime after David. Verse 63 has been added to explain why Jerusalem has not appeared in the city

⁵⁵Maon, Carmel, Ziph, Juttah ⁵⁶Jezreel, Jokdeam, Zanoah, ⁵⁷Kain, Gibbeah and Timnah; ten cities and their villages. ⁵⁸Halhul, Beth-zur, Gedor, ⁵⁹Ma-arath, Beth-anoth and Eltekon; six cities and their villages. Tekoa, Ephrathah (that is, Bethlehem), Peor, Etam, Kulom, Tatam, Zores, Karim, Gallim, Bether and Manoko; eleven cities and their villages. ⁶⁰Kiriath-baal (that is, Kiriath-jearim) and Rabbah: two cities and their villages.

⁶¹In the desert: Beth-arabah, Middin, Secacah, ⁶²Nibshan, Ir-hamelah and En-gedi; six cities and their villages. ⁶³[But the Jebusites who lived in Jerusalem the Judahites could not drive out; so the Jebusites dwell in Jerusalem beside the Judahites to the present day.]

16 The Joseph Tribes. ¹The lot that fell to the Josephites extended from the Jordan at Jericho to the waters of Jericho east of the desert; then the boundary went up from Jericho to the heights at Bethel. ²Leaving Bethel for Luz, it crossed the ridge to the border of the Archites at Ataroth, ³and descended westward to the border of the Japhletites, to that of Lower Beth-horon, and to Gezer, ending thence at the sea.

Ephraim. ⁴Within the heritage of Manasseh and Ephraim, sons of Joseph, ⁵the dividing line for the heritage of the clans of the Ephraimites ran from east of Ataroth-addar to Upper Beth-horon ⁶and

thence to the sea. From Michmethath on the north, their boundary curved eastward around Taanath-shiloh, and continued east of it to Janoah; ⁷from there it descended to Ataroth and Naarah, and skirting Jericho, it ended at the Jordan. ⁸From Tappuah the boundary ran westward to the Wadi Kanah and ended at the sea. This was the heritage of the clans of the Ephraimites, ⁹including the villages that belonged to each city set aside for the Ephraimites within the territory of the Manassehites. ¹⁰But they did not drive out the Canaanites living in Gezer, who live on within Ephraim to the present day, though they have been impressed as laborers.

17 Manasseh. ¹Now as for the lot that fell to the tribe of Manasseh as the first-born of Joseph: since his eldest son, Machir, the father of Gilead, was a warrior, who had already obtained Gilead and Bashan, ²the allotment was now made to the other descendants of Manasseh, the clans of Abiezer, Helek, Asriel, Shechem, Hepher and Shemida, the other male children of Manasseh, son of Joseph.

³Furthermore, Zelophehad, son of Hepher, son of Gilead, son of Machir, son of Manasseh, had had no sons, but only daughters, whose names were Mahlah, Noah, Hoglah, Milcah, and Tirzah. ⁴These presented themselves to Eleazar

---

list, namely, because the Judahites could not drive out the Jebusites who lived in the city. It will be David who eventually captures the city (2 Sam 5:6-9).

16:1–17:18 Allotment to the Joseph tribes. This section is made up of four parts: a broad description of the area occupied by the Josephites, in which the Josephites are presented as one tribe (vv. 1-3); a list of the boundaries of the tribe of Ephraim (vv. 4-10); a list of the allotment made to the descendants of Manasseh, other than Machir, who had already obtained land east of the Jordan (17:1-13); and a story of how Joseph's descendants complained that they needed more land (17:14-18).

These lists are in obvious contrast to the detailed Judahite lists in the previous chapters. Fewer details are given and the material is often presented

the priest, to Joshua, son of Nun, and to the princes, saying, "The LORD commanded Moses to give us a heritage among our kinsmen." So in obedience to the command of the LORD a heritage was given to each of them among their father's kinsmen. ⁵Thus ten shares fell to Manasseh apart from the land of Gilead and Bashan beyond the Jordan, ⁶since these female descendants of Manasseh received each a portion among his sons. The land of Gilead fell to the rest of the Manassehites.

⁷Manasseh bordered on Asher. From Michmethath, near Shechem, another boundary ran southward to include the natives of En-Tappuah, ⁸because the district of Tappuah belonged to Manasseh, although Tappuah itself was an Ephraimite city on the border of Manasseh. ⁹This same boundary continued down to the Wadi Kanah. The cities that belonged to Ephraim from among the cities of Manasseh were those to the south of the wadi; thus the territory of Manasseh ran north of the wadi and ended at the sea. ¹⁰The land on the south belonged to Ephraim and that on the north to Manasseh; with the sea as their common boundary, they reached Asher on the north and Issachar on the east.

¹¹Moreover, in Issachar and in Asher Manasseh was awarded Beth-shean and its towns, Ibleam and its towns, Dor and its towns and the natives there, Endor and its towns and natives, Taanach and its towns and natives, and Megiddo and its towns and natives [the third is Naphathdor]. ¹²Since the Manassehites could not conquer these cities, the Canaanites persisted in this region. ¹³When the Israelites grew stronger they impressed the Canaanites as laborers, but they did not drive them out.

Protest of Joseph Tribes. ¹⁴The descendants of Joseph said to Joshua, "Why have you given us only one lot and one share as our heritage? Our people are too many, because of the extent to which the LORD has blessed us." ¹⁵Joshua answered them, "If you are too many, go up to the forest and clear out a place for yourselves there in the land of the Perizzites and Rephaim, since the mountain regions of Ephraim are so narrow." ¹⁶For the Josephites said, "Our mountain regions are not enough for us; on the other hand, the Canaanites living in the valley region all have iron chariots, in particular those in Beth-shean and its towns, and those in the valley of Jezreel." ¹⁷Joshua therefore said to Ephraim and Manasseh, the house

in a very confused way. Notice the concern to explain why Canaanites continued to live in the midst of these tribes (16:10; 17:12), though in both cases it is insisted that the Canaanites were eventually impressed as laborers, even if they were not driven out.

In verses 1-6 we find delineated, by means of a genealogical formulation, the members of the half-tribe of Manasseh, who settled in the area west of the Jordan (see Num 26:28-34). The clan of Machir (v. 1) made up the half-tribe that settled east of the Jordan.

Verses 14-18 consist of two versions (14-15; 16-18) of the same tradition combined into one narrative. The theme of both is a request by Joseph's descendants for more territory, because the hill country they had been given was not large enough to accommodate all of them. In verses 16-18 they also complain that they had been unable to drive out the Canaanites because of their iron chariots. In both versions Joshua responds by telling the Josephites

of Joseph, "You are a numerous people and very strong. You shall have not merely one share, ¹⁸for the mountain region which is now forest shall be yours when you clear it. Its adjacent land shall also be yours if, despite their strength and iron chariots, you drive out the Canaanites."

18 ¹After they had subdued the land, the whole community of the Israelites assembled at Shiloh, where they set up the meeting tent.

The Seven Remaining Portions. ²Seven tribes among the Israelites had not yet received their heritage. ³Joshua therefore said to the Israelites, "How much longer will you put off taking steps to possess the land which the Lord, the God of your fathers, has given you? ⁴Choose three men from each of your tribes; I will commission them to begin a survey of the land, which they shall describe for pur-

poses of inheritance. When they return to me, ⁵you shall divide it into seven parts. Judah is to retain its territory in the south, and the house of Joseph its territory in the north. ⁶You shall bring here to me the description of the land in seven sections. I will then cast lots for you here before the Lord, our God. ⁷For the Levites have no share among you, because the priesthood of the Lord is their heritage; while Gad, Reuben, and the half-tribe of Manasseh have already received the heritage east of the Jordan which Moses, the servant of the Lord, gave them."

⁸When those who were to map out the land were ready for the journey, Joshua instructed them to survey the land, prepare a description of it, and return to him; then he would cast lots for them there before the Lord in Shiloh. ⁹So they went through the land, listed its cities in writing in seven sections, and returned to

to make better use of their hill country by clearing out some of the forest. In the second version he also encourages them to overcome the Canaanites.

18:1–19:51 Allotment at Shiloh. Having presented the allotment of land to the major tribes of Judah and Joseph, the editor, after an introduction (18:1-10), describes the allotments to the seven remaining tribes: Benjamin (18:11-28); Simeon (19:1-9); Zebulun (19:10-16); Issachar (19:17-23); Asher (19:24-31); Naphtali (19:32-39).

The introduction (18:1-10) describes the procedure of allotting the land: after a representative body (three members from each tribe) surveys and prepares a description of it, the land is divided into seven parts. Joshua assigns the various parts to the seven tribes by casting lots, but it is highly unlikely that the tribes actually received their land in this way. In reality the process was a highly complex one of historical settlement over a period of time. Note that whereas the tribes of Judah and Joseph initiated the procedure for getting their allotment, Joshua is pictured here (v. 3) as admonishing the other seven tribes for not taking more initiative in possessing the subdued land. The reference to Shiloh is probably secondary, since the reference to Judah in the south and Joseph in the north (v. 5) does not make sense if the reference point is Shiloh, which was in the territory of Ephraim. The original tradition supposed Gilgal as the place for this allotment of land. Historically, Shiloh succeeded Gilgal as the national shrine. The reference to the meeting

Joshua in the camp at Shiloh. [10]Joshua then divided up the land for the Israelites into their separate shares, casting lots for them before the LORD in Shiloh.

Benjamin. [11]One lot fell to the clans of the tribe of Benjaminites. The territory allotted them lay between the descendants of Judah and those of Joseph. [12]Their northern boundary began at the Jordan and went over the northern flank of Jericho, up westward into the mountains, till it reached the desert of Beth-aven. [13]From there it crossed over to the southern flank of Luz (that is, Bethel). Then it ran down to Ataroth-addar, on the mountaintop south of Lower Beth-horon. [14]For the western border, the boundary line swung south from the mountaintop opposite Beth-horon till it reached Kiriath-baal (that is, Kiriath-jearim), which city belonged to the Judahites. This was the western boundary. [15]The southern boundary began at the limits of Kiriath-jearim and projected to the spring at Nephtoah. [16]It went down to the edge of the mountain on the north of the Valley of Rephaim, where it faces the Valley of Ben-hinnom; and continuing down the Valley of Hinnom along the southern flank of the Jebusites, reached En-rogel. Inclining to the north, it extended to En-shemesh, and thence to Geliloth, opposite the pass of Adummim. Then it dropped to Eben-Bohan-ben-Reuben, [18]across the northern flank of the Arabah overlook, down into the Arabah. [19]From there the boundary continued across the northern flank of Beth-hoglah and extended to the northern tip of the Salt Sea, at the southern end of the Jordan. This was the southern boundary. [20]The Jordan bounded it on the east. This was how the heritage of the clans of the Benjaminites was bounded on all sides.

[21]Now the cities belonging to the clans of the tribe of the Benjaminites were: Jericho, Beth-hoglah, Emek-keziz, [22]Betharabah, Zemaraim, Bethel, [23]Avvim, Parah, Ophra, [24]Chephar-ammoni, Ophni and Geba; twelve cities and their villages. [25]Also Gibeon, Ramah, Beeroth, [26]Mizpeh, Chephirah, Mozah, [27]Rekem, Irpeel, Taralah, [28]Zela, Haeleph, the Jebusite city (that is, Jerusalem), Gibeah and Kiriath; fourteen cities and their villages. This was the heritage of the clans of Benjaminites.

19 **Simeon.** [1]The second lot fell to Simeon. The heritage of the clans of the tribe of Simeonites lay within that of the Judahites. [2]For their heritage they received Beer-sheba, Shema, Moladah, [3]Hazar-shual, Balah, Ezem, [4]Eltolad, Bethul, Hormah, [5]Ziklag, Bethmarcaboth, Hazar-susah, [6]Beth-lebaoth and Sharuhen; thirteen cities and their villages. [7]Also En-rimmon, Ether and Ashan; four cities and their villages, [8] besides all the villages around these cities as far as Baalath-beer (that is, Ramothnegeb). This was the heritage of the clans of the tribe of the Simeonites. [9]This

---

tent (v. 1) is curious, since references to the meeting tent are very rare in the Deuteronomistic sections of the Old Testament (see Deut 31:14-15; 1 Sam 2:22). This reference to the meeting tent is probably due to a later editing of the text.

In general the allotments given to the different tribes are described in terms of ancient boundary lists and city lists drawn up for administrative purposes. Notice that for Simeon (19:1-9) no tribal boundaries are given. The reason is that from a very early period the tribe of Simeon was absorbed into the tribe of Judah and had no territory of its own. Rather, Simeon occupied cer-

heritage of the Simeonites was within the confines of the Judahites; for since the portion of the latter was too large for them, the Simeonites obtained their heritage within it.

Zebulun. ¹⁰The third lot fell to the clans of the Zebulunites. The limit of their heritage was at Sarid. ¹¹Their boundary went up west . . . and through Mareal, reaching Dabbesheth and the wadi that is near Jokneam. ¹²From Sarid eastward it ran to the district of Chisloth-tabor, on to Daberath, and up to Japhia. ¹³From there it continued eastward to Gath-hepher and to Eth-kazin, extended to Rimmon, and turned to Neah. ¹⁴Skirting north of Hannathon, the boundary ended at the valley of Iphtahel. ¹⁵Thus, with Kattath, Nahalal, Shimron, Idalah and Bethlehem, there were twelve cities and their villages ¹⁶to comprise the heritage of the clans of the Zebulunites.

Issachar. ¹⁷The fourth lot fell to Issachar. The territory of the clans of the Issacharites ¹⁸included Jezreel, Chesulloth, Shunem, ¹⁹Hapharaim, Shion, Anaharath, ²⁰Rabbith, Kishion, Ebez, ²¹Remeth, En-gannim, En-haddah and Beth-pazzez. ²²The boundary reached Tabor, Shahazumah and Beth-shemesh, ending at the Jordan. These sixteen cities and their villages ²³were the heritage of the clans of the Issacharites.

Asher. ²⁴The fifth lot fell to the clans of the tribe of the Asherites. ²⁵Their territory included Helkath, Hali, Beten, Achshaph, ²⁶Allammelech, Amad and Mishal, and reached Carmel on the west,

and Shihor-libnath. ²⁷In the other direction, it ran eastward of Beth-dagon, reached Zebulun and the valley of Iphtahel; then north of Beth-emek and Neiel, it extended to Cabul, ²⁸Mishal, Abdon, Rehob, Hammon and Kanah, near Greater Sidon. ²⁹Then the boundary turned back to Ramah and to the fortress city of Tyre; thence it cut back to Hosah and ended at the sea. Thus, with Mahalab, Achzib, ³⁰Ummah, Acco, Aphek and Rehob, there were twenty-two cities and their villages ³¹to comprise the heritage of the clans of the tribe of the Asherites.

Naphtali. ³²The sixth lot fell to the Naphtalites. The boundary of the clans of the Naphtalites ³³extended from Heleph, from the oak at Zaanannim to Lakkum, including Adami-nekeb and Jabneel, and ended at the Jordan. ³⁴In the opposite direction, westerly, it ran through Aznoth-tabor and from there extended to Hukkok; it touched Zebulun on the south, Asher on the west, and the Jordan on the east. ³⁵The fortified cities were Ziddim, Zer, Hammath, Rakkath, Chinnereth, ³⁶Adamah, Ramah, Hazor, ³⁷Kedesh, Edrei, En-hazor, ³⁸Yiron, Migdal-el, Horem, Beth-anath and Beth-shemesh; nineteen cities and their villages, ³⁹to comprise the heritage of the clans of the tribe of the Naphtalites.

Dan. ⁴⁰The seventh lot fell to the clans of the tribe of Danites. ⁴¹Their heritage was the territory of Zorah, Eshtaol, Ir-shemesh, ⁴²Shaalabbin, Aijalon, Ithlah, ⁴³Elon, Timnah, Ekron, ⁴⁴Eltekoh, Gib-

---

tain cities within the area belonging to Judah. D justifies this allotment to the Simeonites on the basis that Judah's portion was larger than it needed to be.

Seemingly, the original allotment to Dan was very small. However, the main reason the Danites were forced to migrate north (v. 47) was because they could not conquer the Canaanites in the coastal plain that was part of their original allotment (see Judg 17–18).

bethon, Baalath, ⁴⁵Jehud, Bene-berak, Gath-rimmon, ⁴⁶Me-jarkon and Rakkon, with the coast at Joppa. ⁴⁷But the territory of the Danites was too small for them; so the Danites marched up and attacked Leshem, which they captured and put to the sword. Once they had taken possession of Leshem, they renamed the settlement after their ancestor Dan. ⁴⁸These cities and their villages were the heritage of the clans of the tribe of the Danites.

Joshua's City. ⁴⁹When the last of them had received the portions of the land they were to inherit, the Israelites assigned a heritage in their midst to Joshua, son of Nun. ⁵⁰In obedience to the command of the LORD, they gave him the city which he requested, Timnah-serah in the mountain region of Ephraim. He rebuilt the city and made it his home.

⁵¹These are the final portions into which Eleazar the priest, Joshua, son of Nun, and the heads of families in the tribes of the Israelites divided the land by lot in the presence of the LORD, at the door of the meeting tent in Shiloh.

20 **Cities of Asylum.** ¹The LORD SAID to Joshua: ²"Tell the Israelites to designate the cities of which I spoke to them through Moses, ³to which one guilty of accidental and unintended homicide may flee for asylum from the avenger of blood. ⁴To one of these cities the killer shall flee, and standing at the entrance of the city gate, he shall plead his case before the elders, who must receive him and assign him a place in which to live among them. ⁵Though the avenger of blood pursues him, they are not to deliver up the homicide who slew his fellow man unintentionally and not out of previous hatred. ⁶Once he has stood judgment before the community, he shall live on in that city till the death of the high priest who is in office at the time. Then the killer may go back home to his own city from which he fled.

List of Cities. ⁷So they set apart Kedesh in Galilee in the mountain region of Naphtali, Shechem in the mountain region of Ephraim, and Kiriath-arba (that is, Hebron) in the mountain region of

That Joshua was granted a specific city as his own is reported only here. Perhaps the passage (vv. 49-50) was added to justify the later statement that Joshua was buried within his own heritage (Josh 24:30; Judg 2:9).

The conclusion to this section is based on 14:1 and 18:1.

20:1-9 The cities of asylum. The right of sanctuary is an ancient tradition that is found in both classical and oriental antiquity and is normally associated with certain sanctuaries. This passage lists those cities where a person who has accidentally killed another could find refuge and asylum. Behind this passage is the fact that in ancient semitic society, in the case of murder, it was the responsibility of the victim's next of kin to avenge the death by taking the life of the murderer. This was true even in the case of an accidental killing. Hence, there was a need to protect a person who accidentally killed another. Cities of asylum have no parallel that we are aware of. The six cities that are listed here show up again in the list of Levitical cities in chapter 21, and Shechem and Hebron housed famous sanctuaries. That a sanctuary also existed at Kedesh (the name means "holy") is also probable. Therefore, it would seem that the right of asylum is connected with these cities because of the sanctuaries located in them.

Judah. ⁸And beyond the Jordan east of Jericho they designated Bezer on the open tableland in the tribe of Reuben, Ramoth in Gilead in the tribe of Gad, and Golan in Bashan in the tribe of Manasseh. ⁹These were the designated cities to which any Israelite or stranger living among them who had killed a person accidentally might flee to escape death at the hand of the avenger of blood, until he could appear before the community.

21 **Levitical Cities.** ¹The heads of the Levite families came up to Eleazar the priest, to Joshua, son of Nun, and to the heads of families of the other tribes of the Israelites ²at Shiloh in the land of Canaan, and said to them, "The LORD commanded, through Moses, that cities be given us to dwell in, with pasture lands for our livestock. ³Out of their own heritage, in obedience to this command of the LORD, the Israelites gave the Levites the following cities with their pasture lands.

⁴When the first lot among the Levites fell to the clans of the Kohathites, the descendants of Aaron the priest obtained thirteen cities by lot from the tribes of Judah, Simeon and Benjamin. ⁵The rest of the Kohathites obtained ten cities by lot from the clans of the tribe of Ephraim, from the tribe of Dan, and from the half-tribe of Manasseh. ⁶The Gershonites ob-

tained thirteen cities by lot from the clans of the tribe of Issachar, from the tribe of Asher, from the tribe of Naphtali, and from the half-tribe of Manasseh. ⁷The clans of the Merarites obtained twelve cities from the tribes of Reuben, Gad and Zebulun. ⁸These cities with their pasture lands the Israelites allotted to the Levites in obedience to the LORD's commmand through Moses.

Cities of the Priests. ⁹From the tribes of the Judahites and Simeonites they designated the following cities, ¹⁰and assigned them to the descendants of Aaron in the Kohathite clan of the Levites, since the first lot fell to them: ¹¹first, Kiriatharba (Arba was the father of Anak), that is, Hebron, in the mountain region of Judah, with the adjacent pasture lands, ¹²although the open country and villages belonging to the city had been given to Caleb, son of Jephunneh, as his property. ¹³Thus to the descendants of Aaron the priest were given the city of asylum for homicides at Hebron, with its pasture lands; also, Libnah with its pasture lands, ¹⁴Jattir with its pasture lands, Eshtemoa with its pasture lands, ¹⁵Holon with its pasture lands, Debir with its pasture lands, ¹⁶Ashan with its pasture lands, Juttah with its pasture lands, and Beth-shemesh with its pasture lands: nine cities from the two tribes mentioned.

A difficulty with the picture this chapter presents is that, aside from the laws concerning this custom of asylum in Num 35:9-15 and Deut 19:1-13, no biblical text provides a concrete example of its practice. So, serious questions may be raised about the historicity of what is presented here, and no sufficient evidence is available to give any satisfactory answers.

21:1-42 Levitical cities. D has pointed out several times that the tribe of Levi received no heritage, i.e., no block of territory (13:14, 33; 14:4; 18:7). The Levites received only cities to live in along with their pasture lands (14:4). This chapter lists those cities that were given to the Levites in fulfillment of the Lord's command to Moses (Num 35:1-8).

The major issue regarding the chapter is whether the institution of the Levitical cities is historically true. The list of cities as we have it is artificially

[17]From the tribe of Benjamin they obtained the four cities of Gibeon with its pasture lands, Geba with its pasture lands, [18]Anathoth with its pasture lands, and Almon with its pasture lands. [19]These cities which with their pasture lands belonged to the priestly descendants of Aaron, were thirteen in all.

Cities of the Other Kohathites. [20]The rest of the Kohathite clans among the Levites obtained by lot, from the tribe of Ephraim, four cities. [21]They were assigned, with its pasture lands, the city of asylum for homicides at Shechem in the mountain region of Ephraim; also Gezer with its pasture lands, [22]Kibzaim with its pasture lands, and Beth-horon with its pasture lands. [23]From the tribe of Dan they obtained the four cities of Elteke with its pasture lands, Gibbethon with its pasture lands, [24]Aijalon with its pasture lands, and Gath-rimmon with its pasture lands; [25]and from the half-tribe of Manasseh the two cities of Taanach with its pasture lands and Ibleam with its pasture lands. [26]These cities which with their pasture lands belonged to the rest of the Kohathite clans were ten in all.

Cities of the Gershonites. [27]The Gershonite clan of the Levites received from the half-tribe of Manasseh two cities: the city of asylum for homicides at Golan with its pasture lands; and also Beth-Astharoth with its pasture lands. [28]From the tribe of Issachar they obtained the four cities of Kishion with its pasture lands, Daberath with its pasture lands, [29]Jarmuth with its pasture lands, and Engannim with its pasture lands; [30]from the tribe of Asher, the four cities of Mishal with its pasture lands, Abdon with its pasture lands, [31]Helkath with its pasture lands, and Rehob with its pasture lands; [32]and from the tribe of Naphtali, three cities: the city of asylum for homicides at Kedesh in Galilee, with its pasture lands; also Hammath with its pasture lands, and Rakkath with its pasture lands. [33]These cities which with their pasture lands belonged to the Gershonite clans were thirteen in all.

Cities of the Merarites. [34]The Merarite clans, the last of the Levites, received from the tribe of Zebulun the four cities of Jokneam with its pasture lands, Kartah with its pasture lands, [35]Rimmon with

arranged, as is apparent in the twelve-tribe scheme imposed upon it. Again, we see nowhere in the Old Testament any concrete example of how this institution functioned. It is not surprising, then, that some see the institution of Levitical cities, and hence this list, as purely theoretical and idealistic. However, there are scholars today who claim that there is a historical reality underlying the story. Specifically they say that the Levitical cities represent "colonies," i.e., places assigned to faithful groups like the Levites in order to bring stability to a given area. Others argue that the list represents an administrative arrangement established by David for governing the frontier areas of his new empire. It is true that Israel controlled the extensive territory presupposed by the list only in the time of David and Solomon, and the majority of the cities listed here are known to have been difficult frontier areas of the empire conquered by David. The Levites were not the only inhabitants of these cities, but they did have certain prerogatives and rights regarding these cities and their pasture lands.

its pasture lands, and Nahalal with its pasture lands; ³⁶also, across the Jordan, from the tribe of Reuben, four cities: the city of asylum for homicides at Bezer with its pasture lands, Jahaz with its pasture lands, ³⁷Kedemoth with its pasture lands, and Mephaath with its pasture lands; ³⁸and from the tribe of Gad a total of four cities: the city of asylum for homicides at Ramoth in Gilead with its pasture lands, also Mahanaim with its pasture lands, ³⁹Heshbon with its pasture lands, and Jazer with its pasture lands. ⁴⁰The cities which were allotted to the Merarite clans, the last of the Levites, were therefore twelve in all.

⁴¹Thus the total number of cities within the territory of the Israelites which, with their pasture lands, belonged to the Levites, was forty-eight. ⁴²With each and every one of these cities went the pasture lands round about it.

⁴³And so the LORD gave Israel all the land he had sworn to their fathers he would give them. Once they had conquered and occupied it, ⁴⁴the LORD gave them peace on every side, just as he had promised their fathers. Not one of their enemies could withstand them; the LORD brought all their enemies under their power. ⁴⁵Not a single promise that the LORD made to the house of Israel was broken; every one was fulfilled.

III: RETURN OF THE TRANSJORDAN TRIBES AND JOSHUA'S FAREWELL

22 The Eastern Tribes Dismissed. ¹At that time Joshua summoned the Reubenites, the Gadites, and the half-tribe of Manasseh ²and said to them: "You have done all that Moses, the servant of the LORD, commanded you, and

The story of the origin of the Levites as descendants of the three sons of Levi (Kohath, Gershon and Merari) is both late (post-exilic) and an over-simplification of the reality. Notice that the Kohathites are divided into two groups: the descendants of Aaron (the priests) and the other Kohathites.

21:43–22:34 Conclusion. These verses conclude the narrative of the division of the land (21:43–22:9) and provide an appendix regarding the building of a great altar by the Transjordanian tribes on their return to their own lands (22:10-34).

21:43–22:9 Summary and dismissal of the eastern tribes. Verses 43-45 are a summary of the books up to this point. This summary, like the others noted in the book (9:1-2; 10:40-43), goes beyond what has actually been reported in the individual stories that precede it. Despite allusions to the contrary (13:1-6), the editor claims here that Israel has conquered all of the land. What is important, however, is the message that the editor wishes to convey here, namely, that the Lord has been faithful to all the promises made to the patriarchs. As a result Israel has taken possession of all the land and has found peace. As we have noted, this is the major theme of the Book of Joshua and an important message for the people in exile in the sixth century. The exiles can trust this God who is faithful to past promises and who has the power to fulfill them.

The material in 22:1-9 is closely linked to 21:43-45 because it is the "peace" described in 21:45 that permits the dismissal of the eastern tribes reported

have obeyed every command I gave you. ³For many years now you have not once abandoned your kinsmen, but have faithfully carried out the commands of the LORD, your God. ⁴Since, therefore, the LORD, your God, has settled your kinsmen as he promised them, you may now return to your tents beyond the Jordan; to your own land, which Moses, the servant of the LORD, gave you. ⁵But be very careful to observe the precept and law which Moses, the servant of the LORD, enjoined upon you: love the LORD, your God, follow him faithfully; keep his commandments; remain loyal to him; and serve him with your whole heart and soul." ⁶Joshua then blessed them and sent them away to their own tents.

⁷(For, to half the tribe of Manasseh Moses had assigned land in Bashan; and to the other half Joshua had given a portion along with their kinsmen west of the Jordan.) What Joshua said to them when he sent them off to their tents with his blessing was, ⁸"Now that you are returning to your own tents with great wealth, with very numerous livestock, with silver, gold, bronze and iron, and with a very large supply of clothing, divide these spoils of your enemies with your kinsmen there." ⁹So the Reubenites, the Gadites, and the half-tribe of Manasseh left the other Israelites at Shiloh in the land of Canaan and returned to the land of Gilead, their own property, which they had received according to the LORD's command through Moses.

The Altar beside the Jordan. ¹⁰When the Reubenites, the Gadites, and the half-tribe of Manasseh came to the region of the Jordan in the land of Canaan, they built there at the Jordan a conspicuously large altar. ¹¹The other Israelites heard the report that the Reubenites, the Gadites, and the half-tribe of Manasseh had built an altar in the region of the Jordan facing the land of Canaan, across from them, ¹²and therefore they assembled their whole community at Shiloh to declare war on them.

Accusation of the Western Tribes. ¹³First, however, they sent to the Reubenites, the Gadites, and the half-tribe of Manasseh in the land of Gilead an em-

in 22:1-9. These verses frame the theme developed in 1:12-18. Joshua acknowledges the fidelity of the eastern tribes (vv. 1-3) and, because the tribes west of the Jordan are settled, he dismisses the eastern tribes so that they can return to their own lands (v. 4) with the admonition to remain faithful to the law of Moses (v. 5). He then sends them on their way with his blessing (v. 6). The editor gives special attention to the eastern tribes throughout the book in order to emphasize that the conquest of the land was the work of all Israel. The unity of all of the tribes was quite important to the editor.

22:10-34 Appendix: The construction of the great altar. This story constitutes an appendix to the narrative of the conquest and division of the land. On the surface it tells of how, on their way home, the eastern tribes construct a very large altar in the region of the Jordan River (v. 10). When the other tribes hear of this, they meet to declare war on the eastern tribes (vv. 11-12). The reason for such a strong reaction to the altar is found in the accusation of the delegation sent to get an explanation, namely, the altar is seen as an act of rebellion against the Lord (v. 16). The objecting tribes are fearful of the ramifications of this sin upon all of the tribes (vv. 17-20). What

bassy consisting of Phinehas, son of Eleazar the priest, [14]and ten princes, one from every tribe of Israel, each one being both prince and military leader of his ancestral house. [15]When these came to the Reubenites, the Gadites, and the half-tribe of Manasseh in the land of Gilead, they said to them: [16]"The whole community of the LORD sends this message: What act of treachery is this you have committed against the God of Israel? You have seceded from the LORD this day, and rebelled against him by building an altar of your own! [17]For the sin of Peor, a plague came upon the community of the LORD. [18]We are still not free of that; must you now add to it? You are rebelling against the LORD today and by tomorrow he will be angry with the whole community of Israel! [19]If you consider the land you now possess unclean, cross over to the land the LORD possesses, where the Dwelling of the LORD stands, and share that with us. But do not rebel against the LORD, nor involve us in rebellion, by building an altar of your own in addition to the altar of the LORD, our God. [20]When Achan, son of Zerah, violated the ban, did not wrath fall upon the entire community of Israel? Though he was but a single man, he did not perish alone for his guilt!"

Reply of the Eastern Tribes. [21]The Reubenites, the Gadites, and the half-tribe of Manasseh replied to the military leaders of the Israelites: "The LORD is the God of gods. [22]The LORD, the God of gods, knows and Israel shall know. If now we have acted out of rebellion or treachery against the LORD, our God, [23]and if we have built an altar of our own to secede from the LORD, or to offer holocausts, grain offerings or peace offerings upon it, the LORD himself will exact the penalty. [24]We did it rather out of our anxious concern lest in the future your children should say to our children: 'What have you to do with the LORD, the God of Israel? [25]For the LORD has placed the Jordan as a boundary between you and us. You descendants of Reuben and Gad have no share in the LORD.' Thus your children would prevent ours from revering the LORD. [26]So we decided to guard our interests by building this altar of our own: not for holocausts or for sacrifices, [27]but as evidence for you on behalf of ourselves and our descendants, that we have the right to worship the LORD in his presence with our holocausts, sacrifices, and peace offerings. Now in the future your children cannot say to our children, 'You have no share in the LORD.' [28]Our thought was, that if in the future they should speak thus to us or to our descendants, we could answer: 'Look at the model of the altar of the LORD which our fathers made, not for holocausts or for sacrifices, but to witness between you and us.' [29]Far be it from us to rebel against the LORD or to secede now from the LORD by building an altar for holocaust, grain offering, or sacrifice in addition to the altar of the LORD, our God, which stands before his Dwelling."

is presupposed here is the belief of the D editor that there can be only one place of worship. The western tribes are mollified when the eastern tribes assure them that the altar is not meant for sacrifices but for a memorial—a reminder to all the tribes that the eastern tribes, though not living in the Promised Land, strictly speaking (see v. 19), did have a right to worship the Lord (vv. 21-29).

Behind the story stands an older narrative that probably dealt with some conflict between the eastern and western tribes over religious practices, and

³⁰When Phinehas the priest and the princes of the community, the military leaders of the Israelites, heard what the Reubenites, the Gadites and the Manassehites had to say, they were satisfied. ³¹Phinehas, son of Eleazar the priest, said to the Reubenites, the Gadites and the Manassehites, "Now we know that the LORD is with us. Since you have not committed this act of treachery against the LORD, you have kept the Israelites free from punishment by the LORD."

³²Phinehas, son of Eleazar the priest, and the princes returned from the Reubenites and the Gadites in the land of Gilead to the Israelites in the land of Canaan, and reported the matter to them. ³³The report satisfied the Israelites, who blessed God and decided against declaring war on the Reubenites and Gadites or ravaging the land they occupied.

³⁴The Reubenites and the Gadites gave the altar its name as a witness among them that the LORD is God.

23 **Joshua's Final Plea.** ¹Many years later, after the LORD had given the Israelites rest from all their enemies round about them, and when Joshua was old and advanced in years, ²he summoned all Israel (including their elders, leaders, judges and officers) and said to them: "I

which provided an etiology to describe some great altar. The story has been so thoroughly reworked, that it is impossible to say anything about the original narrative. As it stands, it is a clear warning against illegitimate cultic places, and it stresses the unity of all the tribes. This latter point is found in the concept of corporate guilt expressed in verses 17-20, where the presumed treachery of the eastern tribes is understood to affect all of the tribes, and in the reason given by the eastern tribes for building the altar—as witness to the unity of the eastern and western tribes.

It is not clear from verses 10 and 11 if the altar was built on the western or eastern side of the Jordan. For the story of Peor, see Num 25:6-18. The thrust of the remark in verse 18 would seem to imply that Israel is still offering sacrifices to atone for that sin.

PART III: JOSHUA'S FAREWELL AND DEATH

Josh 23:1–24:33

23-24 Joshua's farewell address. Though these two chapters have separate introductions, they go together in the final edition of the book as the last will and testament of Joshua. Joshua, realizing that his end is near, gathers the people together to remind them of all that has taken place and to encourage them to be faithful to the covenant. He also warns them of the dire consequences of rebellion against the Lord.

Both chapters must be seen against the background of ancient Near Eastern treaties. Scholars are aware of strong parallels between the way the covenant at Sinai is presented in the Old Testament and the form of ancient Near Eastern vassal treaties. These treaties usually contained the following

am old and advanced in years. ³You have seen all that the LORD, your God, has done for you against all these nations; for it has been the LORD, your God, himself who fought for you. ⁴Bear in mind that I have apportioned among your tribes as their heritage the nations that survive [as well as those I destroyed] between the Jordan and the Great Sea in the west. ⁵The LORD, your God, will drive them out and dislodge them at your approach, so that you will take possession of their land as the LORD, your God, promised you. ⁶Therefore strive hard to observe and carry out all that is written in the book of the law of Moses, not straying from it in any way, ⁷or mingling with these nations while they survive among you. You

elements: self-introduction by the sovereign; a recounting of history, i.e., what the sovereign has done for the vassal; stipulations that the vassal is to observe as a response to what the sovereign has done for him; blessings and curses for fidelity, or lack thereof, to the treaty; calling upon witnesses; and a demand that the treaty be read periodically before the people. These elements, in different ways, give shape to these two chapters.

23:1-16 Joshua's final plea. This chapter falls into the category of a farewell address. Joshua recalls the past, especially God's actions on behalf of the people, reminds the people of what the Lord asks of them, and of what must still be done. The address has been affected by the style of the Levitical sermon, in which there is much repetition and a mixture of history, stipulation, curses, and blessings. In these latter elements one sees the influence of the ancient vassal treaties.

The chapter is a total creation of the D author, and forms the conclusion to the narrative of the conquest. The purpose of the chapter is to explain to the exiles why they have lost the land, namely, because of their disloyalty to Yahweh, which has brought about the fulfillment of the Lord's threats of destruction. By emphasizing that the Lord has fulfilled all the promises made in the past (vv. 2-11), the author is telling the people that if they again turn to the Lord, they can have their land back; because the Lord is faithful to past promises. Through specific warnings in the text, the author is telling the exiles how they must act in their present situation.

After the Lord has given the Israelites rest from all their enemies, Joshua, in his old age, summons Israel for his farewell address (vv. 1-2). He recalls all that the Lord has done for the people (v. 3), points out that in accord with the promises that have been made, the Lord will drive out the nations before the Israelites from the regions allotted them (vv. 4-5), and calls the people to obedience to the law of Moses (vv. 6-8). The people are to avoid any activity that might even imply the existence of the gods of the foreigners (v. 7). Then the author once again recalls how the Lord drove out the nations before Israel (v. 9) out of fidelity to the promises made in the past (v. 10), and calls Israel to love the Lord (v. 11). Joshua threatens Israel: if

must not invoke their gods, or swear by them, or serve them, or worship them, ⁸but you must remain loyal to the LORD, your God, as you have been to this day. ⁹At your approach the LORD has driven out large and strong nations, and to this day no one has withstood you. ¹⁰One of you puts to flight a thousand, because it is the LORD, your God, himself who fights for you, as he promised you. ¹¹Take great care, however, to love the LORD, your God. ¹²For if you ever abandon him and ally yourselves with the remnant of these nations while they survive among you, by intermarrying and intermingling with them, ¹³know for certain that the LORD, your God, will no longer drive these nations out of your way. Instead they will be a snare and a trap for you, a scourge for your sides and thorns for your eyes, until you perish from this good land which the LORD, your God, has given you.

¹⁴"Today, as you see, I am going the way of all men. So now acknowledge with your whole heart and soul that not one of all the promises of the LORD, your God, made to you has remained unfulfilled. Every promise has been fulfilled for you, with not one single exception. ¹⁵But just as every promise the LORD, your God, made to you has been fulfilled for you, so will he fulfill every threat, even so far as to exterminate you from this good land which the LORD, your God, has given you. ¹⁶If you transgress the covenant of the LORD, your God, which he enjoined on you, serve other gods and worship them, the anger of the LORD will flare up against you and you will quickly perish from the good land which he has given you."

24 **Reminder of the Divine Goodness.** ¹Joshua gathered together all the tribes of Israel at Shechem, summoning their elders, their

she abandons Yahweh and in any way allies herself with the foreign nations (v. 12), then the Lord will no longer drive out the nations before her, but will abandon her to the nations (v. 13). Israel is to acknowledge that every promise of the Lord has been fulfilled (v. 14). Joshua points out that as the Lord has fulfilled all the promises made in the past, so also will the Lord fulfill every threat, namely, to exterminate Israel from the land if she transgresses the covenant (vv. 15-16).

24:1-28 Renewal of the covenant. In contrast to chapter 23 this chapter is based on a tradition that contains authentic memories of ancient covenant renewal ceremonies. The dating of this covenant ceremony to the end of Joshua's life is provided only by the context—not by the report itself. These verses are closely related to the ceremony on Mount Ebal reported in 8:30-35 and, historically, would fit better into that context than at the end of Joshua's life.

While the text may be rooted in some past ceremony, such as a renewal of the Sinai covenant in which the Shechemites were invited to participate, the present text has been influenced by covenant renewal ceremonies that were celebrated periodically in Israel. These ceremonies in turn had been influenced by the form of the ancient Near Eastern vassal treaties.

leaders, their judges and their officers. When they stood in ranks before God, ²Joshua addressed all the people: "Thus says the LORD, the God of Israel: In times past your fathers, down to Terah, father of Abraham and Nahor, dwelt beyond the River and served other gods. ³But I brought your father Abraham from the region beyond the River and led him through the entire land of Canaan. I made his descendants numerous, and gave him Isaac. ⁴To Isaac I gave Jacob and Esau. To Esau I assigned the mountain region of Seir in which to settle, while Jacob and his children went down to Egypt.

⁵"Then I sent Moses and Aaron, and smote Egypt with the prodigies which I wrought in her midst. ⁶Afterward I led you out of Egypt, and when you reached the sea, the Egyptians pursued your fathers to the Red Sea with chariots and horsemen. ⁷Because they cried out to the LORD, he put darkness between your people and the Egyptians, upon whom he brought the sea so that it engulfed them. After you witnessed what I did to Egypt, and dwelt a long time in the desert, ⁸I brought you into the land of the Amorites who lived east of the Jordan. They fought against you, but I delivered them into your power. You took possession of their land, and I destroyed them [the two kings of the Amorites] before you. ⁹Then Balak, son of Zippor, king of Moab, prepared to war against Israel. He summoned Balaam, son of Beor, to curse you; ¹⁰but I would not listen to Balaam. On the contrary, he had to bless you, and I saved you from him. ¹¹Once you crossed the Jordan and came to Jericho, the men of Jericho fought against you, but I delivered them also into your power. ¹²And I sent the hornets ahead of you which drove them [the Amorites, Perizzites, Canaanites, Hittites, Girgashites, Hivites and Jebusites] out of your way; it was not your sword or your bow.

¹³"I gave you a land which you had not tilled and cities which you had not built, to dwell in; you have eaten of vineyards and olive groves which you did not plant. ¹⁴"Now, therefore, fear the LORD and serve him completely and sincerely. Cast out the gods your fathers served beyond the River and in Egypt, and serve the LORD. ¹⁵If it does not please you to serve the LORD, decide today whom you will serve, the gods your fathers served beyond the River or the gods of the Amorites in whose country you are dwelling. As for me and my household, we will serve the LORD."

Joshua gathers together all the tribes of Israel at Shechem in order to address them (v. 1). Shechem, an ancient cultic center, is near the present town of Nablus, about 30 miles north of Jerusalem. No information is available on how Israel came into control of the central hill country where Shechem is located. It was probably a peaceful occupation. Joshua now addresses the people (vv. 2-15). The major part of the address is a recitation of Israel's history from the time of the patriarchs to the period of the conquest (vv. 2-13). Joshua stresses that it was the Lord who was responsible for all that had taken place.

The river referred to in verses 2 and 3 is the Euphrates, and the mountain region of Seir (v. 4) refers to the area south of the Dead Sea. The land of the Amorites (v. 8) is the region east of the Jordan. On Balaam, see Num 22–24. Verse 14 contains the stipulation of the covenant: total commitment to Yahweh because of all that Yahweh had done for them. Verse 15 contains

Renewal of the Covenant. [16]But the people answered, "Far be it from us to forsake the LORD for the service of other gods. [17]For it was the LORD, our God, who brought us and our fathers up and out of the land of Egypt, out of a state of slavery. He performed those great miracles before our very eyes and protected us along our entire journey and among all the peoples through whom we passed. [18]At our approach the LORD drove out [all the peoples, including] the Amorites who dwelt in the land. Therefore we also will serve the LORD, for he is our God."

[19]Joshua in turn said to the people, "You may not be able to serve the LORD, for he is a holy God; he is a jealous God who will not forgive your transgressions or your sins. [20]If, after the good he has done for you, you forsake the LORD and serve strange gods, he will do evil to you and destroy you."

[21]But the people answered Joshua, "We will still serve the LORD." [22]Joshua therefore said to the people, "You are your own witnesses that you have chosen to serve the LORD." They replied, "We are, indeed!" [23]"Now, therefore, put away the strange gods that are among you and turn your hearts to the LORD, the God of Israel." [24]Then the people promised Joshua, "We will serve the LORD, our God, and obey his voice."

[25]So Joshua made a covenant with the people that day and made statutes and ordinances for them at Shechem, [26]which he recorded in the book of the law of God. Then he took a large stone and set it up there under the oak that was in the sanctuary of the LORD. [27]And Joshua said to all the people, "This stone shall be our

Joshua's challenge to the people: decide whom you will serve! The response of the people (vv. 16-18) is that they, as Joshua's household, will serve the Lord because of all that the Lord has done for them.

In response to the warning of Joshua about the implications of disloyalty (vv. 19-20), the people reaffirm their commitment (v. 21). Following upon the declaration of witnesses (v. 22), the people solemnly profess their willingness to serve the Lord in response to Joshua's invitation (vv. 23-24). The covenant is then made, a large stone is set up to commemorate the event, and the people are dismissed (vv. 25-28). The function of the stone is not clear. It is possible that the terms of the covenant were written upon it, but this is not said.

In its present context the purpose of this chapter is clear. The author is calling the exiles to total loyalty to the Lord in response to all that the Lord has done for them. As the original Israelites had committed themselves to Yahweh, so now must the Israelites in exile choose whom they will serve. By reporting the renewal of the covenant the editor also makes it clear to the exiles that the covenant can be renewed again if Israel is willing to commit herself completely to Yahweh as her ancestors had done. The threat about the response of the Lord to Israel's infidelity (vv. 19-20) is meant to remind the Israelites once again that the reason they had lost their land was because of their disobedience.

witness, for it has heard all the words which the LORD spoke to us. It shall be a witness against you, should you wish to deny your God." ²⁸Then Joshua dismissed the people, each to his own heritage.

Death of Joshua. ²⁹Ater these events, Joshua, son of Nun, servant of the LORD, died at the age of a hundred and ten. ³⁰He was buried within the limits of his heritage at Timnath-serah in the mountain region of Ephraim north of Mount Gaash. ³¹Israel served the LORD during the entire lifetime of Joshua and that of the elders who outlived Joshua and knew all that the LORD had done for Israel. ³²The bones of Joseph, which the Israelites had brought up from Egypt, were buried in Shechem in the plot of ground Jacob had bought from the sons of Hamor, father of Shechem, for a hundred pieces of money. This was a heritage of the descendants of Joseph. ³³When Eleazar, son of Aaron, also died, he was buried on the hill which had been given to his son Phinehas in the mountain region of Ephraim.

24:29-31 The death of Joshua. After a long life Joshua dies and is buried at Timnath-serah, the Ephraimite town that had been given to him for his services (19:49-50). Verse 31 serves as a transition to the Book of Judges.

24:32-33 Burial traditions. Someone else has added these brief notes about the reburial of the bones of Joseph at Shechem (see Gen 50:25 and 33:19), and the burial of Eleazar, the contemporary of Joshua.

The Book of Judges

Introduction

The Book of Judges tells the story of Israel between the death of Joshua and the rise of Samuel. The core of the book is a collection of stories about several heroes from Israel's past—the judges. Attached to the stories are various traditions concerning the period before the monarchy.

The book is in three sections: a prologue (1:1–2:5); stories of the judges (2:6–16:31); and an appendix dealing with the migration of the tribe of Dan and the civil war against Benjamin (17:1–21:25).

The judges

The book is named for its major protagonists who are said to have "judged" Israel. The writer distinguishes between the "major" judges and the "minor" judges. The major judges are charismatic military leaders, the subjects of extended narratives. The minor judges are those about whom little information is given beyond their names and the length of their office.

The Hebrew verb that is normally translated as "judge" has two basic meanings: to exercise the function of a judge (in the context of a court or in private judgment) and to rule. None of the judges are ever associated with any function of judgment or arbitration except for Deborah (4:4-5); but this is before she is called by God. Rather, the major judges are shown exercising a specifically military role and sometimes acting as civil rulers. No information is provided on the activity of the minor judges.

Another title that is used for several of the judges is "savior," probably the original title of at least some of the judges. The major judges are presented as charismatics, i.e., people who are raised up by the spirit of the Lord to deliver the people from oppression. Whatever power is given to them is seen as an exceptional measure.

Composition of the book

The book is a series of stories about Israelite heroes who had delivered the people from oppression. The stories originally told of the deliverance of individual tribes and so were limited in their geographical scope. Only later were the heroes made into deliverers of all Israel. These heroic tales from the folklore of the people were meant to entertain and edify, and had been collected together before the Deuteronomistic Historian (D) decided to make use of them. (On the work of the Deuteronomistic Historian, see the introduction to the Book of Joshua.)

It was probably D who gave these heroes their pan-Israelite orientation. D also imposed a theological framework on the stories of the major judges. This framework provides an introduction that describes how the people have sinned; how God has allowed them to fall into the hands of their enemies; and how, when the people cried out, the Lord sent a savior to deliver them. Each story ends with a note about how long the land was at peace as a result of the deliverance effected by each savior-judge. D's framework provides the key for interpreting the stories of the judges, i.e., how sin leads to punishment, but repentance leads to deliverance.

The purpose of the Book of Judges

The Book of Judges must be read in the context of the Deuteronomistic History. The author's purpose is to present a basic theology of history: sin leads to punishment, but repentance brings forgiveness and deliverance. This message was meant for the people in exile who had recently lost their land. The author is explaining to them that they had lost the land because of their sinfulness; but, if they now repent and turn back to the Lord, the Lord will once again forgive them and deliver them. While a message of hope is present, the book as a whole shows the progressive intensification of the sin of the people. The occasion of this sin is what is presented in the first chapter, namely, that Israel did not drive out of the land the nations with their idolatrous practices. As one goes through the book, the disastrous consequences of this situation become more and more apparent.

Historical accuracy

The basic traditions about the major judges, the material about the conquest in chapter 1, and the reports on the activities of the tribes of Dan and Benjamin in the appendix are quite old. The later Deuteronomistic editors did not significantly rework these stories, but confined themselves to adding comments at the beginning and end of them and inserting connectives between the stories. There is no reason to deny that the stories are based on real events, though each tradition must be studied separately in terms of its historicity. Just because the stories are old does not mean that they can be accepted uncritically as historical.

Later editors modified two aspects of the stories by imposing the "pan-Israel" perspective on them and by adopting an artificial chronology. As we mentioned above, the "pan-Israel" perspective was introduced at a later time on stories that originally spoke of the deliverance of a limited number of tribes. The chronology found in the book is another matter. If one counts up all the years mentioned in the text, then the period of the judges would cover 410 years, obviously much too long, since the evidence available places the period of the judges somewhere between 1200 B.C. and 1050 B.C., approximately 150 years. A close reading clearly shows that the chronology in the book is stereotyped and artificial. D has imposed the chronology to support the comment in 1 Kgs 6:1 that there were 480 years between the Exodus and the beginning of the construction of the Jerusalem temple. Though the book shows the judges as following one after the other, in reality some of the major judges could have been contemporaries. The sequence chronology is demanded by having each of the judges be a deliverer of all Israel.

The Book of Judges

Text and Commentary

I: PALESTINE AFTER THE DEATH OF JOSHUA

1 **Pagan Survivors in Palestine.** [1]After the death of Joshua the Israelites consulted the LORD, asking, "Who shall be first among us to attack the Canaanites and to do battle with them?" [2]The LORD answered, "Judah shall attack: I have delivered the land into his power." [3]Judah then said to his brother Simeon, "Come up with me into the territory allotted to me, and let us engage the Canaanites in battle. I will likewise accompany you into the territory allotted to you." So Simeon went with him.

PART I: THE CONQUEST

Judg 1:1–2:5

This section presents a different view of the conquest of Palestine from the one presented in Josh 1–12. Here there is no acquaintance with the idea of a comprehensive conquest of Palestine by a united army of Israel. Rather, the picture is that of each tribe, alone or with one or two others, struggling to carve out a territory for itself.

The chapter is not a unified literary composition, but has been built up from separate traditions, many of which are quite old, and which come from different sources than the traditions used in Josh 1–12. The material has been arranged to describe the activity of the various tribes on a line from south to north. The Israel presented here is unable to occupy the coastal plains either in the south or in the central part of the country, and is unable to control the plain of Jezreel. As a result, the people are cut off from the great fertile areas of the land. This seems to be more in keeping with the archaeological evidence than the picture presented in Joshua.

However, it is important to see that the editor has not introduced this material either to counter or correct the picture in Joshua, but rather as a report on the activities of the generation after the death of Joshua but during the lifetime of the elders who outlived him. This is clear from the fact that 1:1-3, which come from D, presuppose the singular view of the conquest found in Joshua and the allotment of the land reported in Josh 13–22, and that the material in 2:10 refers to the generation that followed after the elders who survived Joshua. The editor, then, has introduced this prologue to prepare for the negative evaluation of the period that is found in 2:1-5. Chapter 1 is, therefore, intended to provide the basis for the explanation in

⁴When the forces of Judah attacked, the LORD delivered the Canaanites and Perizzites into their power, and they slew ten thousand of them in Bezek. ⁵It was in Bezek that they came upon Adonibezek and fought against him. When they defeated the Canaanites and Perizzites, ⁶Adonibezek fled. They set out in pursuit, and when they caught him, cut off his thumbs and his big toes. ⁷At this Adonibezek said, "Seventy kings, with their thumbs and big toes cut off, used to pick up scraps under my table. As I have done, so has God repaid me." He was brought to Jerusalem, and there he died.

⁸[The Judahites fought against Jerusalem and captured it, putting it to the sword; then they destroyed the city by fire.]

⁹Afterward the Judahites went down to fight against the Canaanites who lived in the mountain region, in the Negeb, and in the foothills. ¹⁰Judah also marched against the Canaanites who dwelt in Hebron, which was formerly called Kiriath-arba, and defeated Sheshai, Ahiman and Talmai. ¹¹From there they marched against the inhabitants of Debir, which was formerly called Kiriath-sepher. ¹²And Caleb said, "I will give my daughter Achsah in marriage to the one

2:1-5 of why the Israelites would not be able to clear out the inhabitants of the land from their midst, namely, because they had disobeyed the Lord by making pacts with the inhabitants of the land, and by not pulling down their altars. As a result the Lord will not clear these nations out of Israel's way but will leave them in the land so that they can oppose Israel, and so that their gods will become a snare for Israel (2:3).

As the book opens, the editor seems to presuppose that Israel is still at Gilgal (see 2:1 and Josh 4:19; 10:43; 14:6; and the comments on Josh 18:5). Now that the land has been subdued and apportioned among the tribes (see Joshua), it is necessary for each tribe to lay claim to its territory. They consult the Lord to see who will be the first to attack the Canaanites (1:1). The Lord's response is that Judah shall be first, and Judah invites Simeon to join them (vv. 2-3). This association shows that the tribe of Simeon was absorbed into the tribe of Judah at a very early period, and had no territory of its own (see Josh 19:1-9).

Verses 4-36 present the successes and failures of the various tribes. The fact that Judah is presented first and given such a large amount of space (vv. 4-20) shows that the editor presupposed the preeminence of the tribe of Judah. To a large extent Judah is successful in its encounters with the inhabitants of the land, but not completely (see vv. 18-20). The Perizzites (v. 4) were part of the indigenous population of Palestine (see Josh 17:15 and Gen 34:30). The incident with Adonibezek at Bezek is reminiscent of the story of Adonizedek in Josh 10 and may be related. The location of Bezek is uncertain. Adonibezek's mutilation is intended to humiliate him and render him incapable of war in the future. Verse 8, concerning the capture of Jerusalem, appears to be a later insertion into the text and does not agree with verse 21. The material in verses 10-15 is basically a duplicate of Josh

who attacks Kiriath-sepher and captures it." ¹³Othniel, son of Caleb's younger brother Kenaz, captured it; so Caleb gave him his daughter Achsah in marriage. ¹⁴On the day of her marriage to Othniel she induced him to ask her father for some land. Then, as she alighted from the ass, Caleb asked her, "What is troubling you?" ¹⁵"Give me an additional gift," she answered. "Since you have assigned land in the Negeb to me, give me also pools of water." So Caleb gave her the upper and the lower pool. ¹⁶The descendants of the Kenite, Moses' father-in-law, came up with the Judahites from the city of palms to the desert at Arad [which is in the Negeb]. But they later left and settled among the Amalekites.

¹⁷Judah then went with his brother Simeon, and they defeated the Canaanites who dwelt in Zephath. After having doomed the city to destruction, they renamed it Hormah. ¹⁸Judah, however, did not occupy Gaza with its territory, Ashkelon with its territory, or Ekron with its territory. ¹⁹Since the LORD was with Judah, he gained possession of the mountain region. Yet he could not dislodge those who lived on the plain, because they had iron chariots. ²⁰As Moses had commanded, Hebron was given to Caleb, who then drove from it the three sons of Anak.

²¹The Benjaminites did not dislodge the Jebusites who dwelt in Jerusalem, with the result that the Jebusites live in Jerusalem beside the Benjaminites to the present day. ²²The house of Joseph, too, marched up against Bethel, and the LORD was with them. ²³The house of Joseph had a reconnaissance made of Bethel, which formerly was called Luz. ²⁴The scouts saw a man coming out of the city and said to him. "Show us a way into the city, and we will spare you." ²⁵He showed them a way into the city, which they then put to the sword; but they let the man and his whole clan go free. ²⁶He then went to the land of the Hittites, where he built a city and called it Luz, as it is still called.

²⁷Manasseh did not take possession of Beth-shean with its towns or of Taanach with its towns. Neither did he dislodge the inhabitants of Dor and its towns, those of Ibleam and its towns, or those of Megiddo and its towns. The Canaanites kept their hold in this district. ²⁸When the Israelites grew stronger, they impressed the Canaanites as laborers, but did not drive them out. ²⁹Similarly, the Ephraimites did not drive out the Canaanites living in Gezer, and so the Canaanites live in Gezer in their midst.

³⁰Zebulun did not dislodge the inhabitants of Kitron or those of Nahalol;

15:13-19, and is meant to explain why the Othnielites had access to the pools of water that should have belonged to the Calebites in Hebron. The reference to the Kenites in verse 16 explains their presence among the tribes of Judah. Judah is unable to take control of the southern coastal plain because the people there had iron chariots (vv. 18-19). The Benjaminites are mentioned next (v. 21) because of their close association with the tribe of Judah. Jerusalem will not be taken until David personally conquers it.

The editor now presents the attack on the central part of the country by the house of Joseph (vv. 22-29). Note that the house of Joseph is shown capturing Bethel, even though the city has been allotted to Benjamin (Josh 18:22). The story (vv. 22-26) is probably meant to illustrate how Israel made pacts with the inhabitants of the land. Verses 27-29 tell of the tribes being unable

the Canaanites live among them, but have become forced laborers.

³¹Nor did Asher drive out the inhabitants of Acco or those of Sidon, or take possession of Mahaleb, Achzib, Helbah, Aphik or Rehob. ³²The Asherites live among the Canaanite natives of the land, whom they have not dislodged.

³³Naphtali did not drive out the inhabitants of Beth-shemesh or those of Beth-anath, and so they live among the Canaanite natives of the land. However, the inhabitants of Beth-shemesh and Beth-anath have become forced laborers for them.

³⁴The Amorites hemmed in the Danites in the mountain region, not permitting them to go down into the plain. ³⁵The Amorites had a firm hold in Harheres, Aijalon and Shaalbim, but as the house of Joseph gained the upper hand, they were impressed as laborers.

³⁶The territory of the Amorites extended from the Akrabbim pass to Sela and beyond.

2 Infidelities of the Israelites. ¹An angel of the LORD went up from Gilgal to Bochim and said, "It was I who brought you up from Egypt and led you into the land which I promised on oath

to take control of the central coastal plain or the plain of Jezreel. These verses, along with the references to the failures in the north (vv. 30-35), are reported as examples of how Israel sinned by living among the original inhabitants of the land instead of driving them out. Notice that it is not said that they could not drive out the natives but that they did not; rather, they put the natives into forced labor.

In 2:1-5 the editor gives the reason for the survey in chapter 1, namely, to explain why in the stories that follow, Israel will be unable to drive out the native inhabitants of the land: because Yahweh will not be with them, since they have been disobedient (see Josh 23:12-13). These verses, composed by D, are the key to the whole section, and send a clear message to the exiles. D is explaining that they have lost the land because they have been disobedient, and have not lived up to the demands of the reform of Josiah (see 2 Kgs 22:1–23:30). The location of Bochim is unknown. Many surmise that the text here originally read "Bethel" (see 20:18, 26; 21:2). The change to "Bochim" in verse 1 supports the etiology of verse 5, where it is explained that the place came to be called Bochim (weepers) because the people wept there. The angel or "messenger" of the Lord is the envoy of the Lord who can speak in the name of the Lord.

PART II: THE JUDGES

Judg 2:6–16:31

2:6–3:6 Introduction. These verses provide the specific introduction to the stories of the judges. Several hands have shared in the formation of this text, which falls into three sections: the report of the death of Joshua (2:6-9);

to your fathers. I said that I would never break my covenant with you, ²but that you were not to make a pact with the inhabitants of this land, and you were to pull down their altars. Yet you have not obeyed me. What did you mean by this? ³For now I tell you, I will not clear them out of your way; they shall oppose you and their gods shall become a snare for you."

⁴When the angel of the Lord had made these threats to all the Israelites, the people wept aloud; ⁵and so that place came to be called Bochim. They offered sacrifice there to the Lord.

⁶When Joshua dismissed the people, each Israelite went to take possession of his own hereditary land. ⁷The people served the Lord during the entire lifetime of Joshua, and of those elders who outlived Joshua, and who had seen all the great work which the Lord had done for Israel. ⁸Joshua, son of Nun, the servant of the Lord, was a hundred and ten years old when he died; ⁹and they buried him within the borders of his heritage at Timnath-heres in the mountain region of Ephraim north of Mount Gaash.

¹⁰But once the rest of that generation were gathered to their fathers, and a later generation arose that did not know the Lord, or what he had done for Israel, ¹¹the Israelites offended the Lord by serving the Baals. ¹²Abandoning the Lord, the

the specific introduction to the stories of the judges (2:10-23); and a list of the nations that remained in the midst of Israel (3:1-6).

2:6-9 The report of the death of Joshua. These verses parallel Josh 24:28-31, but in a different sequence. The repetition shows that Judg 1:1–2:5 is a later insertion into the text for the reasons already given, and to provide a background for understanding the sinfulness of the people and the Lord's judgment upon them as described in 2:10-23. The report of Joshua's death and burial is repeated here to show that a new era has begun.

2:10-23 The specific introduction to the stories of the judges. This material is not unified. It is highly repetitious with an almost identical content found in verses 11-17; 18-19; 20-23. More than likely verse 10 and verses 20-23 were original, D having inserted verses 11-19 later. Their purpose is to show the tremendous apostasy within Israel during the period of the judges. The gods of the native inhabitants have truly become a snare for Israel (see 2:3). Hence, the need for the "saviors," the judges. The verses make clear that in spite of the deliverance that will be brought by the judges, one should not be misled into thinking that the Israelites truly repented of their sinfulness. Rather, the whole period is described as a time of ever-increasing apostasy (2:19).

The author points out that a new era has begun. There is now a generation that has not experienced the Lord's saving deeds on behalf of Israel nor the law of the covenant (v. 10). Rather they have served the pagan god Baal and the Ashtaroth (plural form for various manifestations of the goddess Astarte), abandoning the God of their ancestors who had led them from Egypt, thus provoking the Lord (vv. 11-12). Baal and Astarte (v. 13) were the embodiment of the idolatrous Canaanite cult. The use of the plural "Baals"

God of their fathers, who had led them out of the land of Egypt, they followed the other gods of the various nations around them, and by their worship of these gods provoked the LORD. ¹³Because they had thus abandoned him and served Baal and the Ashtaroth, ¹⁴the anger of the LORD flared up against Israel, and he delivered them over to plunderers who despoiled them. He allowed them to fall into the power of their enemies round about whom they were no longer able to withstand. ¹⁵Whatever they undertook, the LORD turned into disaster for them, as in his warning he had sworn he would do, till they were in great distress. ¹⁶Even when the LORD raised up judges to deliver them from the power of their despoilers, ¹⁷they did not listen to their judges, but abandoned themselves to the worship of other gods. They were quick to stray from the way their fathers had taken, and did not follow their example of obedience to the commandments of the LORD. ¹⁸Whenever the LORD raised up judges for them, he would be with the judge and save them from the power of their enemies as long as the judge lived; it was thus the LORD took pity on their distressful cries of affliction under their oppressors. ¹⁹But when the judge died, they would relapse and do worse than their fathers, following other gods in service and worship, relinquishing none of their evil practices or stubborn conduct.

²⁰In his anger toward Israel the LORD said, "Inasmuch as this nation has violated my covenant which I enjoined on their fathers, and has disobeyed me, ²¹I for my part will not clear away for them any more of the nations which Joshua left

and "Ashtaroth" does not indicate many deities bearing these names but rather the various local forms of them.

This abandonment angers the Lord, and so the Lord allows the people to fall into the power of their enemies (vv. 13-15; see Josh 23:11-13). Even when the Lord raises up judges to deliver them, the people do not listen to them or follow their example of obedience, but continue to worship other gods. And when the judge dies the people relapse and do even worse than before (vv. 16-19). Most scholars believe that D introduced verses 11-19 here to serve as an introduction to the stories of the judges, and that the elements of the theological framework for the stories may be found in them, i.e., the sinfulness of the people, the Lord becoming angry with the people and allowing them to fall into the hands of their enemies, the cry of the people, and the Lord's deliverance. Notice, however, that the third element of the framework, the cry of the people, is only mentioned in passing (v. 18). Also notice that the cry of the people is not one of repentance, but only a cry of distress under affliction (but see 10:6-16). The Lord seems moved more by the suffering of the people than by their repentance. What is revealed here is the Lord's love for and dedication to the people.

The people's sinfulness is so great, however, that the Lord must pass judgment on the people; so the Lord swears not to clear away any more of the nations that Joshua left when he died. These nations will test the Israelites and make them prove again their fidelity to the Lord (vv. 20-23).

69

when he died." ²²Through these nations the Israelites were to be made to prove whether or not they would keep to the way of the LORD and continue in it as their fathers had done; ²³therefore the LORD allowed them to remain instead of expelling them immediately, or delivering them into the power of Israel.

3 ¹The following are the nations which the LORD allowed to remain so that through them he might try all those Israelites who had no experience of the battles with Canaan ²[just to instruct, by training them in battle, those generations only of the Israelites who would not have had that previous experience]: ³the five lords of the Philistines; and all the Canaanites, the Sidonians, and the Hivites who dwell in the mountain region of Lebanon between Baal-hermon and the entrance to Hamath. ⁴These served to put Israel to the test, to determine whether they would obey the commandments the LORD had enjoined on their fathers through Moses. ⁵Besides, the Israelites were living among the Canaanites, Hittites, Amorites, Perizzites, Hivites and Jebusites. ⁶In fact, they took their daughters in marriage, and gave their own daughters to their sons in marriage, and served their gods.

II: STORIES OF THE JUDGES

Othniel. ⁷Because the Israelites had offended the LORD by forgetting the LORD, their God, and serving the Baals and the Asherahs, ⁸the anger of the LORD flared

The message in all of this for the exiles is clear: Israel lost the land because of continuing infidelity to the covenant. However, there is still hope because, as the Lord responded to the cries of distress of the people in the past, so the Lord may do again now. Also, the idea of testing that is emphasized in verse 22 leaves a door open for the exiles—perhaps they can pass the test. The one thing that becomes quite clear from this passage is that God's salvation is a gift; it is not a mechanical response to an action on the part of the people, not even an act of repentance (see 10:10-17).

3:1-6 The nations who remained. These verses give two lists of the nations who remained in the midst of Israel, as well as later reflections on the reason why the Lord left them. The classical listing of the nations who lived in Palestine before the conquest is given in verse 5 (see Josh 3:10). The "five lords of the Philistines" (v. 3) refers to the five cities inhabited by the Philistines (non-Semites who entered Palestine at about the same time as the Israelites) on the southern coastal plain. The added reasons for the Lord leaving the nations in Israel's midst (3:1-2) are intended to be more benevolent than the ones already seen.

3:7-11 Othniel. This report on the first of the judges appears to be constructed by D, and presents an ideal example of D's theology. Because of the generalized nature of the story it is difficult to pin it down to any place or time. Being so short, it helps one to understand clearly the basic elements of D's theology of history.

Israel, forgetting the Lord, serves the Baals and Asherahs (v. 7). This angers the Lord, who delivers the people into the power of Cushan-

up against them, and he allowed them to fall into the power of Cushan-rishathaim, king of Aram Naharaim, whom they served for eight years. ⁹But when the Israelites cried out to the LORD, he raised up for them a savior, Othniel, son of Caleb's younger brother Kenaz, who rescued them. ¹⁰The spirit of the LORD came upon him, and he judged Israel. When he went out to war, the LORD delivered Cushan-rishathaim, king of Aram, into his power, so that he made him subject. ¹¹The land then was at rest for forty years, until Othniel, son of Kenaz, died.

Ehud. ¹²Again the Israelites offended the LORD, who because of this offense strengthened Eglon, king of Moab, against Israel. ¹³In alliance with the Ammonites and Amalekites, he attacked and defeated Israel, taking possession of the city of palms. ¹⁴The Israelites then served Eglon, king of Moab, for eighteen years.

¹⁵But when the Israelites cried out to the LORD, he raised up for them a savior, the Benjaminite Ehud, son of Gera, who was left-handed. It was by him that the Israelites sent their tribute to Eglon, king of Moab. ¹⁶Ehud made himself a two-edged dagger a foot long, and wore it under his clothes over his right thigh. ¹⁷He presented the tribute to Eglon, king of Moab, who was very fat, ¹⁸and after the presentation went off with the tribute bearers. ¹⁹He returned, however, from where the idols are, near Gilgal, and said, "I have a private message for you, O king." And the king said, "Silence!" Then when all his attendants had left his presence, ²⁰and Ehud went in to him

rishathaim, king of Aram Naharaim. When the people cry out to the Lord, the Lord sends them a savior, Othniel, son of Caleb's younger brother, Kenaz (see Josh 15:17). Here in all their simplicity are seen the introductory formulas of D's framework. The location of Aram Naharaim is unknown. The spirit of the Lord that comes upon the judges in these stories connotes an impersonal power or force that so envelops a person that he or she becomes capable of extraordinary deeds. Verse 11 presents D's normal concluding formula.

3:12-30 Ehud. In the story of Ehud one is able to detect for the first time the existence of an ancient tradition that has been taken up and used by the editor. The story begins with D's framework in which Israel sins, the Lord raises up an oppressor, the people cry out, and the Lord sends a savior (vv. 12-15). The story is filled with humor. The oppressor is "Eglon," which means something like "young bull" or "fat calf" (see v. 17). This king with the ridiculous name is slain by the left-handed Benjaminite (Benjamin literally means "son of the right hand") and the king is so fat that the foot-long dagger gets lost in his belly. The story gloats over how the Israelite hero outsmarts the oppressor and his guards. As a result of the deliverance through Ehud, the land is at rest for eighty years (v. 30).

Moab (v. 12) is situated on the southeastern shore of the Dead Sea. Here the king of Moab is shown in alliance with the people from the north (Amorites) and with southern nomads (Amalekites). The setting for this story, however, is the western shore of the Jordan around Jericho (v. 13), confirmed

where he sat alone in his cool upper room, Ehud said, "I have a message from God for you." So the king rose from his chair, ²¹and then Ehud with his left hand drew the dagger from his right thigh, and thrust it into Eglon's belly. ²²The hilt also went in after the blade, and the fat closed over the blade because he did not withdraw the dagger from his body.

²³Then Ehud went out into the hall, shutting the doors of the upper room on him and locking them. ²⁴When Ehud had left and the servants came, they saw that the doors of the upper room were locked, and thought, "He must be easing himself in the cool chamber." ²⁵They waited until they finally grew suspicious. Since he did not open the doors of the upper room, they took the key and opened them. There on the floor, dead, lay their lord!

²⁶During their delay Ehud made good his escape and, passing the idols, took refuge in Seirah. ²⁷On his arrival he sounded the horn in the mountain region of Ephraim, and the Israelites went down from the mountains with him as their leader. ²⁸"Follow me," he said to them, "for the LORD has delivered your enemies the Moabites into your power." So they followed him down and seized the fords of the Jordan leading to Moab, permitting no one to cross. ²⁹On that occasion they slew about ten thousand Moabites, all of them strong and valiant men. Not a man escaped. ³⁰Thus was Moab brought under the power of Israel at that time; and the land had rest for eighty years.

Shamgar. ³¹After him there was Shamgar, son of Anath, who slew six hundred Philistines with an oxgoad. He, too, rescued Israel.

4 Deborah and Barak. ¹After Ehud's death, however, the Israelites again offended the LORD. ²So the LORD allowed them to fall into the power of the Canaanite king, Jabin, who reigned in Hazor. The general of his army was Sisera, who dwelt in Harosheth-ha-goiim.

by the reference to the "cool upper room" (v. 20), appropriate to the desert area around Jericho. The location of Seirah (v. 26) is unknown. Thrown into confusion by the discovery of their dead king, the Moabites attempt to cross the Jordan and return to their home; but the Israelites are ready for them at the fords (vv. 26-29). The story originally dealt only with the tribe of Benjamin in the neighborhood of Jericho (v. 13 "the city of psalms").

3:31 Shamgar. Both the origin and the reason for this reference to Shamgar here in the text is unclear. The reference has no parallel either to the stories of the major judges or to the references to the minor judges. Moreover, it seems to be a late insertion, since 4:1 seems to follow directly on 3:30. The reference to the Philistines as the enemy of Israel is strange here, since they didn't become a problem to Israel until late in the period of the judges. The slaying of the Philistines with an oxgoad recalls the exploits of Samson (15:14-17). Shamgar does not seem to be a Semitic name, and some have surmised that he was really a Canaanite who defeated the Philistines and so delivered Israel.

4:1–5:31 Deborah and Barak. The story of Deborah and Barak is told twice. Chapter 4 is a prose account, while chapter 5 contains a poem celebrating the same victory. Both texts are concerned with a battle between Israel

25 years of love

chico's

CUST# 014130896G

Discount Code: 6302

Passport Club
Don't forget...

We make sure Passport Club members are always the first to know about special sale events, private in-store parties, birthday bonuses, new collections and members-only coupon offers.

And once all of your purchases to-date reach $500, you'll receive Free Basic Shipping to any destination in the continental U.S. and a 5% discount on all merchandise purchases.

So make sure to tell us if you're a Passport member next time you make a purchase. And if you haven't signed up yet...hurry.

Expires October 19, 2008.

25 REASONS WE'RE GLAD WE'RE *not* 25 ANYMORE

....

Help us make the list.

TELL US YOUR REASON WHY LIFE GETS BETTER
AFTER 25, AND WE'LL TELL THE WORLD.

Email us at chicos25reasons@chicos.com.

Please enjoy this exclusive offer:

15% off

your merchandise purchase of $80 or more.

chico's

³But the Israelites cried out to the LORD; for with his nine hundred iron chariots he sorely oppressed the Israelites for twenty years. ⁴At this time the prophetess Deborah, wife of Lappidoth, was judging Israel. ⁵She used to sit under Deborah's palm tree, situated between Ramah and Bethel in the mountain region of Ephraim, and there the Israelites came up to her for judgment. ⁶She sent and summoned Barak, son of Abinoam, from Kedesh of Naphtali. "This is what the LORD, the God of Israel, commands," she said to him; "go, march on Mount Tabor, and take with you ten thousand Naphtalites and Zebulunites. ⁷I will lead Sisera, the general of Jabin's army, out to you at the Wadi Kishon, together with his chariots and troops, and will deliver them into your power." ⁸But Barak answered her,

"If you come with me, I will go; if you do not come with me, I will not go." ⁹"I will certainly go with you," she replied, "but you shall not gain the glory in the expedition on which you are setting out, for the LORD will have Sisera fall into the power of a woman." So Deborah joined Barak and journeyed with him to Kedesh. ¹⁰Barak summoned Zebulun and Naphtali to Kedesh, and ten thousand men followed him. Deborah also went up with him. ¹¹Now the Kenite Heber had detached himself from his own people, the descendants of Hobab, Moses' brother-in-law, and had pitched his tent by the terebinth of Zaanannim, which was near Kedesh.

¹²It was reported to Sisera that Barak, son of Abinoam, had gone up to Mount Tabor. ¹³So Sisera assembled from Harosheth-ha-goiim at the Wadi Kishon

and a strong coalition, perhaps made up of Canaanites and Philistines, near the Wadi Kishon in the valley of Jezreel. Chapter 4 locates this battle on the northern edge of the valley of Jezreel in the neighborhood of Mount Tabor, but chapter 5 locates it more toward the southeastern side of the valley.

4:1-24 The prose narrative. The prose narrative begins with the regular D framework (vv. 1-3). This time the oppressor is the Canaanite king, Jabin, who reigns in Hazor and has a general named Sisera, who lives in Harosheth-ha-goiim. The real actor is Sisera, and the mention of Jabin seems to be secondary, a reference perhaps related to Josh 11:1f. The location of Harosheth-ha-goiim is uncertain, but it would have been in the northern part of Palestine.

Verses 4-10 report the call of Barak through Deborah and his summoning of the tribes of Zebulun and Naphtali for battle. Deborah is described as a prophetess and one to whom people came for judgments (vv. 4-5). She is a judge, then, in the forensic sense. Ramah and Bethel are just a few miles north of Jerusalem. The tribal connections of Deborah are not clear. While she may pass judgments in the mountain regions of Ephraim, she is connected here with the tribes of Zebulun and Naphtali. Barak is from Kedesh, north of Hazor, in the territory of the tribe of Naphtali. The figure of ten thousand men (v. 10) from only two tribes appears to be an exaggeration.

Verse 11 acts as a footnote to prepare for verse 17, explaining how a group of Kenites, who should be located much farther to the south, were to be found in this region.

The fertile plain of Jezreel, with Mount Tabor in the background. On this plain took place the battle between Jabin, king of Hazor, and his allies and the Israelites under Deborah and Barak (Judg 4). Later Gideon was victorious over the Midianites on this same plain (Judg 7). Photo by Makoto Tada, O.S.B.

Close-up view of Mount Tabor.

all nine hundred of his iron chariots and all his forces. ¹⁴Deborah then said to Barak, "Be off, for this is the day on which the LORD has delivered Sisera into your power. The LORD marches before you." So Barak went down Mount Tabor, followed by his ten thousand men. ¹⁵And the LORD put Sisera and all his chariots and all his forces to rout before Barak. Sisera himself dismounted from his chariot and fled on foot. ¹⁶Barak, however, pursued the chariots and the army as far as Harosheth-ha-goiim. The entire army of Sisera fell beneath the sword, not even one man surviving.

¹⁷Sisera, in the meantime, had fled on foot to the tent of Jael, wife of the Kenite Heber, since Jabin, king of Hazor, and the family of the Kenite Heber were at peace with one another. ¹⁸Jael went out to meet Sisera and said to him, "Come in, my lord, come in with me; do not be afraid." So he went into her tent, and she covered him with a rug. ¹⁹He said to her, "Please give me a little water to drink. I am thirsty." But she opened a jug of milk for him to drink, and then covered him over. ²⁰"Stand at the entrance of the tent," he said to her. "If anyone comes and asks, 'Is there someone here?' say, 'No!' " ²¹Instead Jael, wife of Heber, got a tent peg and took a mallet in her hand. While Sisera was sound asleep, she stealthily approached him and drove the peg through his temple down into the ground, so that he perished in death. ²²Then when Barak came in pursuit of Sisera, Jael went out to meet him and said to him, "Come, I will show you the man you seek." So he went in with her, and there lay Sisera dead, with the tent peg through his temple.

²³Thus on that day God humbled the Canaanite king, Jabin, before the Israelites; ²⁴their power weighed ever heavier upon him, till at length they destroyed the Canaanite king, Jabin.

5 Canticle of Deborah. ¹On that day Deborah [and Barak, son of Abinoam] sang this song:

²Of chiefs who took the lead in Israel,
  of noble deeds by the people who
    bless the LORD,
³Hear, O kings! Give ear, O princes!
  I to the LORD will sing my song,

The battle proper is described in verses 12-16, but there is little detail in the report. God is shown as being responsible for everything that happens. The Lord alone is deserving of glory.

The killing of Sisera (vv. 17-22) is a flagrant violation of the law of hospitality. It also appears that Hazor and the clan of Heber, the Kenite, had an alliance with one another! For whatever reason Jael, wife of Heber, decides to stand with the Israelites. Verses 23-24 are the normal D conclusion, though a partial one. D postpones a final chronological reference until 5:31 so as to present chapters 4 and 5 as a unit.

5:1-31 The Canticle of Deborah. Considered one of the oldest texts in the Bible, this poem, because of its age and the condition of its text, is notoriously difficult. The meaning of many early Hebrew words is uncertain and some verses are nearly incomprehensible. Moreover, the connections with chapter 4 are not always clear. In its present form the poem is a song praising Yahweh, the God of Sinai and the conquest, for what the Lord accomplished through Deborah and Barak.

my hymn to the LORD, the God of
Israel.
⁴O LORD, when you went out from Seir,
when you marched from the land of
Edom,
The earth quaked and the heavens were
shaken,
while the clouds sent down showers.
⁵Mountains trembled
in the presence of the LORD, the One
of Sinai,
in the presence of the LORD, the God
of Israel.

⁶In the days of Shamgar, son of Anath,
in the days of slavery caravans
ceased;
Those who traveled the roads
went by roundabout paths.
⁷Gone was freedom beyond the walls,
gone indeed from Israel.

When I, Deborah, rose,
when I rose, a mother in Israel,
⁸New gods were their choice;
then the war was at their gates.
Not a shield could be seen, nor a lance,
among forty thousand in Israel!
⁹My heart is with the leaders of Israel,
nobles of the people who bless the
LORD;
¹⁰They who ride on white asses,
seated on saddlecloths as they go their
way;

¹¹Sing of them to the strains of the harpers
at the wells,
where men recount the just deeds of
the LORD,
his just deeds that brought freedom to
Israel.
¹²Awake, awake, Deborah!
awake, awake, strike up a song.
Strength! arise, Barak,
make despoilers your spoil, son of
Abinoam.
¹³Then down came the fugitives with the
mighty,
the people of the LORD came down for
me as warriors.
¹⁴From Ephraim, princes were in the
valley;
behind you was Benjamin, among
your troops.
From Machir came down commanders,
from Zebulun wielders of the
marshal's staff.

¹⁵With Deborah were the princes of
Issachar;
Barak, too, was in the valley, his
course unchecked.
Among the clans of Reuben
great were the searchings of heart.
¹⁶Why do you stay beside your hearths
listening to the lowing of the herds?
Among the clans of Reuben
great were the searchings of heart!

Originally, verse 1 may have been directly linked to the prayer in verse
31 before the song was inserted. Verse 2 introduces the subject of the song,
namely, the chiefs of Israel and the noble deeds of the people, i.e., what was
accomplished by Deborah and Barak. Verse 3 is an invitation to listen to
this hymn to the God of Israel. Verses 4-5 recall how Yahweh led Israel into
Palestine accompanied by a series of cosmic events. Verses 6-8 describe the
situation before Deborah: it was not safe to travel the roads, people were
worshiping new gods, and Israel was unarmed before foreign armies. Verses
9-11 extend another invitation to sing about the leaders of Israel and about
Yahweh. Verses 12-18 describe the muster of the tribes for the battle that
is to come. Verse 12 describes the general call to Deborah and Barak to muster
the tribes. The gathering of the tribes is described in verse 13, and verses

¹⁷Gilead, beyond the Jordan, rests;
    why does Dan spend his time in
    ships?
Asher, who dwells along the shore,
    is resting in his coves.
¹⁸Zebulun is the people defying death;
    Naphtali, too, on the open heights!
¹⁹The kings came and fought;
    then they fought, those kings of
      Canaan,
At Taanach by the waters of Megiddo;
    no silver booty did they take.
²⁰From the heavens the stars, too,
      fought;
    from their courses they fought against
      Sisera.
²¹The Wadi Kishon swept them away;
    a wadi . . ., the Kishon.
²²Then the hoofs of the horses pounded,
    with the dashing, dashing of his
      steeds.
²³"Curse Meroz," says the Lord,
    "hurl a curse at its inhabitants!
For they came not to my help,
    as warriors to the help of the Lord."
²⁴Blessed among women be Jael,
    blessed among tent-dwelling women.
²⁵He asked for water, she gave him milk;
    in a princely bowl she offered curds.

²⁶With her left hand she reached for the
      peg,
    with her right, for the workman's
      mallet.
She hammered Sisera, crushed his head;
    she smashed, stove in his temple.
²⁷At her feet he sank down, fell, lay still;
    down at her feet he sank and fell;
    where he sank down, there he fell,
      slain.
²⁸From the window peered down and
      wailed
    the mother of Sisera, from the lattice:
"Why is his chariot so long in coming?
    why are the hoofbeats of his chariots
      delayed?"
²⁹The wisest of her princesses answers
      her,
    and she, too, keeps answering herself:
³⁰"They must be dividing the spoil they
      took:
    there must be a damsel or two for
      each man,
Spoils of dyed cloth as Sisera's spoil,
    an ornate shawl or two for me in the
      spoil."
³¹May all your enemies perish thus, O
    Lord!

14-17 describe those tribes who responded positively to the invitation of the Lord and those who did not. Special praise is given to Zebulun and Naphtali in verse 18. Verses 19-22 describe the battle. Behind verses 20-22 there is the idea of a sudden storm that trapped and bogged down Sisera's chariots so that his army was easily defeated.

The events surrounding Sisera's death are reported in verses 23-30. First, the town of Meroz is cursed because, unlike Jael, it did not offer any aid to Israel, perhaps by ignoring the fleeing Sisera. Verses 24-27 gleefully describe the death of Sisera at the hand of Jael. This account is a bit different from what is reported in 4:21. Here Jael appears to hit Sisera as he was drinking the milk. Verses 28-30 report in a mocking way the concern of Sisera's mother over the delay in his return and the response she receives from her wisest princess. Verse 31 summarizes the poem's theology and presents the concluding part of D's framework.

but your friends be as the sun rising in
its might!
And the land was at rest for forty years.

6 **The Call of Gideon.** ¹The Israelites
offended the LORD, who therefore

delivered them into the power of Midian
for seven years, ²so that Midian held
Israel subject. For fear of Midian the
Israelites established the fire signals on the
mountains, the caves for refuge, and the
strongholds. ³And it used to be that when

For the exiles the episode of Deborah and Barak is a strong motivation
to hope and trust in the Lord, who can destroy Israel's enemies and grant
freedom from oppression if Israel will only cry out to the Lord.

6:1–8:28 Gideon. These chapters reiterate the basic cycle of sin, punishment, repentance, and deliverance. This time it is the Midianites who oppress Israel, and the savior sent by the Lord is Gideon. Gideon destroys the
altar of Baal at Ophrah, erects an altar to Yahweh in its place, and receives
a new name, Jerubbaal. With a few men he wins a great victory over the
Midianites, but will not accept the kingship when it is offered to him. While
the narrative appears basically clear and consistent there are many tensions
within it. First of all, there is the double name for the hero, Gideon and Jerubbaal. Secondly, chapter 6 is obviously made up of a series of different traditions (vv. 11-24; 25-32; 33-35; 36-40). There is significant tension between
6:33-35, where all the tribes are mustered, and 7:3-6 where almost immediately most are sent back home for purely theological reasons. In 8:1-3
Ephraim is angry with Gideon because he had not called them, but this seems
directly opposed to what is said in 7:24f. Finally, Gideon is presented not
only as a champion of the people, but also as a man set on vindicating the
death of brothers. All this suggests that the chapters are a collection of
originally independent traditions that have been edited into a continuous
whole, but not skillfully enough to rid the stories of all inconsistencies. Many
of the stories originally concerned only the family of Abiezer from the tribe
of Manasseh, but they were later made to refer to all Israel.

Most scholars accept the historicity of the Israelites oppression by the
Midianites, a people from the desert region southeast of Palestine. Gen 25:2ff.
points out that Midian was a son of Abraham who was sent eastward so
as not to interfere with the inheritance of Isaac. It is not clear here if the
chapters describe just isolated raids, the movement of a seminomadic people
into cultivated areas at certain times of the year, or a full-scale invasion akin
to Israel's own invasion of the land. This issue cannot be solved, but what
is clear is that the editor was more interested in presenting a theological
message to the exiles than in recounting a political and military event.

These chapters fall into four main sections: the call of Gideon (6:1-40);
the defeat of the Midianites (7:1–8:3); the pursuit of the kings of the Midianites
(8:4-21); and the offer of kingship (8:22-28).

the Israelites had completed their sowing, Midian, Amalek and the Kedemites would come up, ⁴encamp opposite them, and destroy the produce of the land as far as the outskirts of Gaza, leaving no sustenance in Israel, nor sheep, oxen or asses. ⁵For they would come up with their livestock, and their tents would become as numerous as locusts; and neither they nor their camels could be numbered, when they came into the land to lay it waste. ⁶Thus was Israel reduced to misery by Midian, and so the Israelites cried out to the LORD.

⁷ When Israel cried out to the LORD because of Midian, ⁸he sent a prophet to the Israelites who said to them, "The LORD, the God of Israel, says: I led you up from Egypt; I brought you out of the place of slavery. ⁹I rescued you from the power of Egypt and of all your other oppressors. I drove them out before you and gave you their land. ¹⁰And I said to you: I, the LORD, am your God; you shall not venerate the gods of the Amorites in whose land you are dwelling. But you did not obey me."

¹¹Then the angel of the LORD came and sat under the terebinth in Ophrah that belonged to Joash the Abiezrite. While his son Gideon was beating out wheat in the wine press to save it from the Midianites, ¹²the angel of the LORD appeared to him and said, "The LORD is with you, O cham-

6:1-40 The call of Gideon. The story of Gideon begins with the standard framework for the stories of the judges. The Midianite oppression is described as being very critical and widespread, extending from central and northern Palestine to the southwest. The Midianites, together with other nomadic peoples, the Amalekites and Kedemites, were rapidly and indiscriminately plundering the countryside. The Israelites were forced into hiding, where they established a series of strongholds and invented a way to signal the approach of the Midianites (vv. 2-5). Reduced to utter misery, the Israelites cry out to the Lord (v. 6). A new element now appears: in response to Israel's cry the Lord sends a prophet to remind the people of all that the Lord had done for them and how the Lord had commanded them not to venerate the pagan gods of the Amorites. But Israel disobeyed the Lord and had indeed worshiped the pagan gods. The point of these verses (vv. 7-10) is the indictment that the Israelites had brought on their own suffering through disobedience, an important message for the audience of the book, the exiles.

The call of Gideon is reported in what appears to be two variant traditions in verses 11-24 and verses 25-32. The first is a cultic legend explaining the origins of the sanctuary at Ophrah, and shows Gideon, a farmer, threshing his wheat in a concealed wine press, in order to hide it from the plunderers. An angel of the Lord appears to Gideon and commissions him to save the people (v. 11). The angel here, as in other places in the Old Testament, represents Yahweh and is interchangeable with Yahweh. Gideon, obviously unaware of the prophet's explanation in verses 7-10, challenges the angel's greeting with a sarcastic remark, claiming that rather than being with him,

pion!" [13]"My Lord," Gideon said to him, "if the LORD is with us, why has all this happened to us? Where are his wondrous deeds of which our fathers told us when they said, 'Did not the LORD bring us up from Egypt?' For now the LORD has abandoned us and has delivered us into the power of Midian." [14]The LORD turned to him and said, "Go with the strength you have and save Israel from the power of Midian. It is I who send you." [15]But he answered him, "Please, my lord, how can I save Israel? My family is the meanest in Manasseh, and I am the most insignificant in my father's house." [16]"I shall be with you," the LORD said to him, "and you will cut down Midian to the last man." [17]He answered him, "If I find favor with you, give me a sign that you are speaking with me. [18]Do not depart from here, I pray you, until I come back to you and bring out my offering and set it before you." He answered, "I will await your return."

[19]So Gideon went off and prepared a kid and an ephah of flour in the form of unleavened cakes. Putting the meat in a basket and the broth in a pot, he brought them out to him under the terebinth and presented them. [20]The angel of God said to him, "Take the meat and unleavened cakes and lay them on this rock; then pour out the broth." When he had done so, [21]the angel of the LORD stretched out the tip of the staff he held, and touched the meat and unleavened cakes. Thereupon a fire came up from the rock which consumed the meat and unleavened cakes, and the angel of the LORD disappeared from sight. [22]Gideon, now aware that it had been the angel of the LORD, said, "Alas, Lord God, that I have seen the angel of the LORD face to face!" [23]The LORD answered him, "Be calm, do not fear. You shall not die." [24]So Gideon built there an altar to the LORD and called it Yahweh-shalom. To this day it is still in Ophrah of the Abiezrites.

[25]That same night the LORD said to him, "Take the seven-year-old spare bullock and destroy your father's altar to Baal and cut down the sacred pole that is by it. [26]You shall build, instead, the proper kind of altar to the LORD, your God, on top

the Lord has abandoned the people (vv. 12-13). Despite Gideon's sarcasm, the Lord appoints him to save Israel (v. 14) and assures him of success because "I will be with you" (vv. 15-16). This interchange reinforces the idea that God alone is responsible for what is about to happen (see ch. 7). Gideon, still not satisfied, asks for a sign, which the Lord gives (vv. 17-21). The sign here is a cultic one in which the deity consumes the offering in a particular way. Consecrated by the fire from the rock, Gideon builds an altar there and calls it "Yahweh-shalom" (vv. 22-24). "Shalom" is a complex word that expresses ideas of peace, cooperation, and agreement between two parties. The idea that seeing Yahweh can be fatal (v. 22) is found several times (e.g., Exod 19:21; 33:18-23).

The story of the destruction of the altar to Baal and the building of a proper altar to Yahweh (vv. 25-32) is a variation of the previous story. The editor has included it here for two reasons: to show that Gideon cannot hope to defeat the enemies of Israel unless he purges out the worship of the foreign gods; and to explain Gideon's other name, his "baal" name, "Jerubbaal," the explanation of which is connected with the people's reaction to Gideon's tear-

of this stronghold. Then take the spare bullock and offer it as a holocaust on the wood from the sacred pole you have cut down." ²⁷So Gideon took ten of his servants and did as the LORD had commanded him. But through fear of his family and of the townspeople, he would not do it by day, but did it at night. ²⁸Early the next morning the townspeople found that the altar of Baal had been destroyed, the sacred pole near it cut down, and the spare bullock offered on the altar that was built. ²⁹They asked one another, "Who did this?" Their inquiry led them to the conclusion that Gideon, son of Joash, had done it. ³⁰So the townspeople said to Joash, "Bring out your son that he may die, for he has destroyed the altar of Baal and has cut down the sacred pole that was near it." ³¹But Joash replied to all who were standing around him, "Do you intend to act in Baal's stead, or be his champion? If anyone acts for him, he shall be put to death by morning. If he whose altar has been destroyed is a god, let him act for

himself!" ³²So on that day Gideon was called Jerubbaal, because of the words, "Let Baal take action against him since he destroyed his altar."

³³Then all Midian and Amalek and the Kedemites mustered and crossed over into the valley of Jezreel, where they encamped. ³⁴The spirit of the LORD enveloped Gideon; he blew the horn that summoned Abiezer to follow him. ³⁵He sent messengers, too, throughout Manasseh, which also obeyed his summons; through Asher, Zebulun and Naphtali, likewise, he sent messengers and these tribes advanced to meet the others. ³⁶Gideon said to God, "If indeed you are going to save Israel through me, as you promised, ³⁷I am putting this woolen fleece on the threshing floor. If dew comes on the fleece alone, while all the ground is dry, I shall know that you will save Israel through me, as you promised."³⁸That is what took place. Early the next morning he wrung the dew from the fleece, squeezing out of it a bowlful of water. ³⁹Gideon then said to God, "Do

ing down the altar of Baal. They want Gideon's father, Joash, to hand him over so they can kill him (vv. 28-30). Joash's response (v. 31) is that if the people act in Baal's place by taking action against Gideon without Baal's authorization, they, too, will be put to death, and if Baal is really a god, he can take care of himself. Gideon's second name is a pun on the Hebrew word which means to "litigate, take action against, sue." Hence, his name means something like "let Baal sue" or "take action."

Verses 33-40 form the transition into the battle with the Midianites described in chapter 7. The Midianites and their allies come across the Jordan from the desert on one of their raids and take control of the valley of Jezreel (v. 33). Originally the story dealt only with the family of Gideon and the family of Abiezer from the tribe of Manasseh, but at some stage in the editing of the material it has become a story about all Israel. Hence, the references here to the tribes of Asher, Zebulun and Naphtali are secondary. Before going into battle Gideon seeks reassurance of divine approval through an oracle (vv. 36-40). Oracles before battle are commonplace in the Old Testament (see e.g., 4:6-7; Josh 6:2-5; 7:10-15; 8:1-2). The use of the fleece may have been an accepted practice. Gideon asks for a second proof, since the first

not be angry with me if I speak once more. Let me make just one more test with the fleece. Let the fleece alone be dry, but let there be dew on all the ground." ⁴⁰That night God did so; the fleece alone was dry, but there was dew on all the ground.

7 Defeat of Midian. ¹Early the next morning Jerubbaal (that is, Gideon) encamped by En-harod with all his soldiers. The camp of Midian was in the valley north of Gibeath-hammoreh. ²The LORD said to Gideon, "You have too many soldiers with you for me to deliver Midian into their power, lest Israel vaunt itself against me and say, 'My own power brought me the victory.' ³Now proclaim to all the soldiers, 'If anyone is afraid or fearful, let him leave.' " When Gideon put them to this test on the mountain, twenty-two thousand of the soldiers left, but ten thousand remained. ⁴The LORD said to Gideon, "There are still too many soldiers. Lead them down to the water and I will test them for you there. If I tell

you that a certain man is to go with you, he must go with you. But no one is to go if I tell you he must not." ⁵When Gideon led the soldiers down to the water, the LORD said to him, "You shall set to one side everyone who laps up the water as a dog does with its tongue; to the other, everyone who kneels down to drink." ⁶Those who lapped up the water raised to their mouths by hand numbered three hundred, but all the rest of the soldiers knelt down to drink the water. ⁷The LORD said to Gideon, "By means of the three hundred who lapped up the water I will save you and will deliver Midian into your power. So let all the other soldiers go home." ⁸Their horns, and such supplies as the soldiers had with them, were taken up, and Gideon ordered the rest of the Israelites to their tents, but kept the three hundred men. Now the camp of Midian was beneath him in the valley.

⁹That night the LORD said to Gideon, "Go, descend on the camp, for I have delivered it up to you. ¹⁰If you are afraid

one may have been inconclusive, i.e., because the fleece could have collected dew even though the ground appeared dry.

7:1–8:3 The defeat of the Midianites. Assured of divine approval for entering into battle, Gideon encamps on a hill above the Midianites' camp. Topographical details in verse 1 are not too clear, but it appears that the opposing forces were encamped toward the southeastern end of the valley of Jezreel. Though the Lord said nothing when Gideon first mustered his troops (6:34-35), the Lord now tells him to reduce the size of his army so that the Israelites will not take credit for the forthcoming victory. The point of 7:1-8 is to show that it is the Lord who is responsible for the victory over the Midianites. The original story described the victory of only three hundred Abiezerites over the Midianites. Later, when the victory was attributed to all Israel, the editors took the opportunity to make the point that God had brought about the victory by having Gideon send all but three hundred warriors home. There are two troop reductions (vv. 3-6). The nature of the test in verses 4-6 is unclear. Why pick the soldiers who lap up the water with their tongues like dogs? It may have been an arbitrary test to provide a means by which God can make a selection. Verse 8 explains how the three hundred get enough jars and horns for use in the battle strategy (see vv. 16-22).

to attack, go down to the camp with your aide Purah. ¹¹When you hear what they are saying, you will have the courage to descend on the camp." So he went down with his aide Purah to the outposts of the camp. ¹²The Midianites, Amalekites, and all the Kedemites lay in the valley, as numerous as locusts. Nor could their camels be counted, for these were as many as the sands on the seashore. ¹³When Gideon arrived, one man was telling another about a dream. "I had a dream," he said, "that a round loaf of barley bread was rolling into the camp of Midian. It came to our tent and struck it, and as it fell it turned the tent upside down." ¹⁴This can only be the sword of the Israelite Gideon, son of Joash," the other replied. "God has delivered Midian and all the camp into his power." ¹⁵When Gideon heard the description and explanation of the dream, he prostrated himself. Then returning to the camp of Israel, he said, "Arise, for the LORD has delivered the camp of Midian into your power."

¹⁶He divided the three hundred men into three companies, and provided them all with horns and with empty jars and torches inside the jars. ¹⁷"Watch me and follow my lead," he told them. "I shall go to the edge of the camp, and as I do, you must do also. ¹⁸When I and those with me blow horns, you too must blow horns all around the camp and cry out, 'For the LORD and for Gideon!' " ¹⁹So Gideon and the hundred men who were with him came to the edge of the camp at the beginning of the middle watch, just after the posting of the guards. They blew the horns and broke the jars they were holding. ²⁰All three companies blew horns and broke their jars. They held the torches in their left hands, and in their right the horns they were blowing, and cried out, "A sword for the LORD and Gideon!" ²¹They all remained standing in place around the camp, while the whole camp fell to running and shouting and fleeing. ²²But the three hundred men kept blowing the horns, and throughout the

Knowing Gideon's need for continued assurances of success, the Lord now takes the initiative and tells him to sneak down to the Midianite camp with his aide and hear what they are saying (vv. 9-11). What is revealed, in contrast to the weakness and fear of Gideon, is the power of the Lord. What Gideon overhears is one man telling another about his dream (vv. 13-14). The point of the loaf of bread symbolizing Israel is to show how small and inadequate the breadloaf is in relation to what it is capable of doing. Once again the point is made that it is the Lord who will be responsible for the victory.

Verses 16-22 describe the attack against the Midianites. Notice that Gideon and his men are not engaged in any fighting; rather, it is the Lord who sets the Midianites against one another (v. 22). Israel divided the night into three watches of four hours apiece. The attack begins at the beginning of the middle watch, about 10:00 p.m. (v. 19). It is hard to imagine how the Israelite soldiers could simultaneously carry out the actions described in verses 19-20. More than likely several different traditions have been combined here. Frightened by the sudden burst of light all around their camp and the noise created by the breaking jars and the horns and the shouts, the Midianites are thrown into disarray and take off toward the east and the Jordan River.

camp the LORD set the sword of one against another. The army fled as far as Beth-shittah in the direction of Zarethan, near the border of Abel-meholah at Tabbath.

²³The Israelites were called to arms from Naphtali, from Asher, and from all Manasseh, and they pursued Midian. ²⁴Gideon also sent messengers throughout the mountain region of Ephraim to say, "Go down to confront Midian, and seize the water courses against them as far as Beth-barah, as well as the Jordan." So all the Ephraimites were called to arms, and they seized the water courses as far as Beth-barah, and the Jordan as well. ²⁵They captured the two princes of Midian, Oreb and Zeeb, killing Oreb at the rock of Oreb and Zeeb at the wine press of Zeeb. Then they pursued Midian and carried the heads of Oreb and Zeeb to Gideon beyond the Jordan.

8 ¹But the Ephraimites said to him, "What have you done to us, not call-ing us when you went to fight against Midian?" And they quarrelled bitterly with him. ²"What have I accomplished now in comparison with you?" he answered them. "Is not the gleaning of Ephraim better that the vintage of Abiezer? ³Into your power God delivered the princes of Midian, Oreb and Zeeb. What have I been able to do in comparison with you?" When he said this, their anger against him subsided.

⁴When Gideon reached the Jordan and crossed it with his three hundred men, they were exhausted and famished. ⁵So he said to the men of Succoth, "Will you give my followers some loaves of bread? They are exhausted, and I am pursuing Zebah and Zalmunna, kings of Midian." ⁶But the princes of Succoth replied, "Are the hands of Zebah and Zalmunna already in your possession, that we should give food to your army?" ⁷Gideon said, "Very well; when the LORD has delivered Zebah and Zalmunna into my

Gideon once again musters the tribes for battle and sends them down to the river fords to intercept the fleeing Midianites as they try to cross the Jordan. Logistically, Gideon's procedure here does not make much sense. He gathers all the tribes and sends all but three hundred home. Then, almost immediately, he turns around and summons the other tribes back. This would have taken time and is not compatible with the speed needed to reach the river fords that is presumed by the text. This tension in the text is the result of making what was originally the victory of one tribe into a victory of all Israel. The summoning of Ephraim in verse 24 does not fit well with the complaint of Ephraim in 8:1-3. Seemingly, the Ephraimites are complaining about the lateness of their summons to battle. The text presupposes that Ephraim was the most important tribe at the time. With good oriental diplomacy Gideon calms down the Ephraimites by quoting a proverb that says how little the family of Abiezer has been able to achieve when compared with what Ephraim has done (vv. 2-3).

8:4-21 The pursuit of the Midianite kings. The focus in this section shifts from the actions of God to the actions of Gideon. Yahweh does not appear in this chapter except for a reference in Gideon's speech (v. 7 and v. 19). The editor may only have wanted to show what became of Gideon. It is not a complimentary picture.

power, I will grind your flesh in with the thorns and briers of the desert." ⁸He went up from there to Penuel and made the same request of them, but the men of Penuel answered him as had the men of Succoth. ⁹So to the men of Penuel, too, he said, "When I return in triumph, I will demolish this tower."

¹⁰Now Zebah and Zalmunna were in Karkor with their force of about fifteen thousand men; these were all who were left of the whole Kedemite army, a hundred and twenty thousand swordsmen having fallen. ¹¹Gideon went up by the route of the nomads east of Nobah and Jogbehah, and attacked the camp when it felt secure. ¹²Zebah and Zalmunna fled. He pursued them and took the two kings of Midian, Zebah and Zalmunna, captive, throwing the entire army into panic. ¹³Then Gideon, son of Joash, returned from battle by the pass of Heres. ¹⁴He

captured a young man of Succoth, who upon being questioned listed for him the seventy-seven princes and elders of Succoth. ¹⁵So he went to the men of Succoth and said, "Here are Zebah and Zalmunna, with whom you taunted me, 'Are the hands of Zebah and Zalmunna already in your possession, that we should give food to your weary followers?' " ¹⁶He took the elders of the city, and thorns and briers of the desert, and ground these men of Succoth into them. ¹⁷He also demolished the tower of Penuel and slew the men of the city.

¹⁸Then he said to Zebah and Zalmunna, "Where now are the men you killed at Tabor?" "They all resembled you," they replied. "They appeared to be princes." ¹⁹"They were my brothers, my mother's sons," he said. "As the LORD lives, if you had spared their lives, I should not kill you." ²⁰Then he said to his

The section begins with a flashback to the situation at 7:22 with Gideon chasing the fleeing Midianites. Both Succoth and Penuel were cities in the Jordan valley, but east of the Jordan River. The reference to the two Midianite kings in verse 5 is surprising, since there has been no previous mention of them. It appears that 8:4-12 may be a variant on 7:22–8:3. The names of the kings are distorted and mean something like "sacrificial victim" and "protection withheld," obvious references to what is going to happen to them. The occupants of Succoth and Penuel are not too convinced that Gideon is going to be victorious and so are not ready to help him, lest they later suffer reprisals from the Midianites (vv. 6-8).

Gideon captures the two kings as they flee from a surprise attack on their camp (vv. 10-12). The location of Karkor is uncertain, but it may have been the central camp from which the Midianites made their periodic raids on Palestine. There is no real proportion in verses 13-17 between the crime and the punishment. Obviously Gideon is attempting to give a message to other people in the area. The "elders of the city" (v. 16) were the governing body when there was no king.

Verses 18-21 come as a real surprise but they explain why Gideon was chasing the two Midianite kings, namely, blood vengeance. They had killed his blood brothers and so now they must be killed. Nothing is known of the incident at Tabor (v. 18) that gave rise to this vendetta.

first-born, Jether, "Go, kill them." Since Jether was still a boy, he was afraid and did not draw his sword. ²¹Zebah and Zalmunna said, "Come, kill us yourself, for a man's strength is like the man." So Gideon stepped forward and killed Zebah and Zalmunna. He also took the crescents that were on the necks of their camels. ²²The Israelites then said to Gideon, "Rule over us—you, your son, and your son's son—for you rescued us from the power of Midian." ²³But Gideon answered them, "I will not rule over you, nor shall my son rule over you. The LORD must rule over you." ²⁴Gideon went on to say, "I should like to make a request of you. Will each of you give me a ring from his booty?" (For being Ishmaelites, the enemy had gold rings.) ²⁵"We will gladly give them," they replied, and spread out a cloak into which everyone threw a ring from his booty. ²⁶The gold rings that he requested weighed seventeen hundred gold shekels, in addition to the crescents and pendants, the purple garments worn by the kings of Midian, and the trappings that were on the necks of their camels. ²⁷Gideon made an ephod out of the gold and placed it in his city Ophrah. However, all Israel paid idolatrous homage to it there, and caused the ruin of Gideon and his family.

²⁸Thus was Midian brought into subjection by the Israelites; no longer did they hold their heads high. And the land had rest for forty years, during the lifetime of Gideon.

Gideon's Son Abimelech. ²⁹Then Jerubbaal, son of Joash, went back home to stay. ³⁰Now Gideon had seventy sons,

8:22-28 Offer of kingship. Originally, Gideon (vv. 22-23) would not have been offered kingship by all of Israel as presented here, but by a more limited group or particular city. As a good follower of Yahweh Gideon refuses the offer and states an orthodox Yahwistic principle: the Lord must rule over you. Though Gideon refuses the title of king, it seems clear from 8:24f. and 9:2f. that he accepts power over the people and demands the trappings of a judge. The ephod made from the booty was a cult object used in obtaining oracles (see Exod 28:15-30). This ephod became an object of idolatrous worship, a practice the editor blames for the eventual downfall of Gideon's family (see ch. 9). Notice how the editor stresses that "all" Israel paid idolatrous homage to the ephod (v. 27). The sinfulness of Israel continues.

8:29–9:57 Abimelech. Though there are some tensions in this material, for the most part the story proceeds with a series of clearly defined scenes. Abimelech, one of Gideon's sons, manages to get himself accepted as king over the city of Shechem by killing all of his brothers except one, Jotham, who invokes a curse upon the city and Abimelech. Tension soon develops between Abimelech and the citizens of Shechem and, as a result of a conspiracy headed by a man named Gaal, military conflict breaks out. Abimelech is victorious, but it is an empty victory. In putting down the revolt he destroys the city, wipes out its citizens, and is killed himself. There is no reason to deny the historicity of the story told here. Shechem was on the southern border of the territory of the tribe of Manasseh in the central highlands and had become part of the Israelite confederacy in the twelfth century. Ar-

his direct descendants, for he had many wives. [31]His concubine who lived in Shechem also bore him a son, whom he named Abimelech. [32]At a good old age Gideon, son of Joash, died and was buried in the tomb of his father Joash in Ophrah of the Abiezrites. [33]But after Gideon was dead, the Israelites again abandoned themselves to the Baals, making Baal of Berith their god [34]and forgetting the LORD, their God, who had delivered them from the power of their enemies all around them. [35]Nor were they grateful to the family of Jerubbaal [Gideon] for all the good he had done for Israel.

9 [1]Abimelech, son of Jerubbaal, went to his mother's kinsmen in Shechem, and said to them and to the whole clan to which his mother's family belonged, [2]"Put this question to all the citizens of Shechem: 'Which is better for you: that

chaeology confirms a significant destruction of the city toward the end of the twelfth century.

The story of Abimelech does not fit the pattern of the other stories of the major judges. First of all, Abimelech is not portrayed as a hero who saves Israel from oppression. Secondly, the D framework is missing, except for the opening statement on the sin of Israel. This passage (8:33-35), along with the conclusion to the story (9:56-57), provides the key for understanding the story. In 8:33-35 Israel is indicted for sinfulness and for being ungrateful to the family of Jerubbaal (Gideon); and in 9:56-57 is found the explanation of the story: it is to show how God requites the evil of Abimelech and the citizens of Shechem who have turned to idolatry and destroyed Gideon's family. In other words, the story is about Israel's sinfulness and punishment. Because it comes immediately after Gideon's refusal of the crown, the story of Abimelech stands out as the tale of the wicked son who accepted the crown—in fact sought it. The story also has a strong anti-monarchy sentiment. The emphasis on sin and punishment is meant especially for the exiles: the reason for the destruction of Jerusalem and the loss of the land in their own time is their sinfulness, especially their following after strange gods.

The all-Israel emphasis in the story is clearly secondary, i.e., added after the fact. Abimelech never ruled over all Israel, but only over the city-state of Shechem and its territories.

The description of Gideon's sons and the note on Gideon's death in 8:29-32 acts as a transition to the story of Abimelech. A concubine (v. 31) is a legitimate wife, but a wife of second rank. The god Baal of Berith (v. 33) was the patron deity of Shechem. By accepting him the people returned to the pre-Israelite form of governance known at Shechem, the monarchy. Rejection of Yahweh is also rejection of a social-political system.

Because Abimelech did not have any right to rule over Shechem, he had to approach the citizens of Shechem through intermediaries, namely, his mother's kinsfolk in Shechem (9:1-3). The "citizens," the prominent people of Shechem who formed a civic assembly, had the power to appoint a per-

seventy men, or all Jerubbaal's sons, rule over you, or that one man rule over you?' You must remember that I am your own flesh and bone." ³When his mother's kin repeated these words to them on his behalf, all the citizens of Shechem sympathized with Abimelech, thinking, "He is our kinsman." ⁴They also gave him seventy silver shekels from the temple of Baal of Berith, with which Abimelech hired shiftless men and ruffians as his followers. ⁵He then went to his ancestral house in Ophrah, and slew his brothers, the seventy sons of Jerubbaal, on one stone. Only the youngest son of Jerubbaal, Jotham, escaped, for he was hidden. ⁶Then all the citizens of Shechem and all Beth-millo came together and proceeded to make Abimelech king by the terebinth at the memorial pillar in Shechem.

⁷When this was reported to him, Jotham went to the top of Mount Gerizim, and standing there, cried out to them in a loud voice: "Hear me, citizens of Shechem, that God may then hear you!

⁸Once the trees went to anoint a king over themselves. So they said to the olive tree, 'Reign over us.' ⁹But the olive tree answered them, 'Must I give up my rich oil, whereby men and gods are honored, and go to wave over the trees?' ¹⁰Then the trees said to the fig tree, 'Come; you reign over us!' ¹¹But the fig tree answered them, 'Must I give up my sweetness and my good fruit, and go to wave over the trees?' ¹²Then the trees said to the vine, 'Come you, and reign over us.' ¹³But the vine answered them, 'Must I give up my wine that cheers gods and men, and go to wave over the trees?' ¹⁴Then all the trees said to the buckthorn, 'Come; you reign over us!' ¹⁵But the buckthorn replied to the trees, 'If you wish to anoint me king over you in good faith, come and take refuge in my shadow. Otherwise, let fire come from the buckthorn and devour the cedars of Lebanon.'

¹⁶"Now then, if you have acted in good faith and honorably in appointing Abimelech your king, if you have dealt

son king. Behind the story lies the fact that even though Gideon did not accept kingship, his sons exercised considerable influence after his death and the citizens of Shechem were unhappy with such a situation. They are willing, therefore, to give Abimelech the money to hire the ruffians he needs to kill his brothers (vv. 4-5). The reference to the "one stone" (v. 5) suggests a public execution of all of them at the same place. The number seventy is a round figure for many. For the sacred oak tree (terebinth) at Shechem see Gen 12:6; Deut 11:30; Josh 24:26.

Jotham's fable (vv. 7-15) has been made to fit here by the addition of verse 15, and reflects a strong rejection of the institution of the monarchy. While the olive, fig, and vine are typical and prized trees in Palestine, the buckthorn, aside from producing beautiful flowers in the spring, seemed worthless to the ancients and a real nuisance because of its thorns. The point of the fable is that only the worst and least qualified are disposed to accept the crown. Jotham's speech (vv. 16-21) is aimed at the citizens of Shechem who have not acted honorably in making Abimelech king, and he utters a curse against both of them. Verses 17-18 are a later addition to the text to explain the statement in verse 16.

well with Jerubbaal and with his family, and if you have treated him as he deserved—[17]for my father fought for you at the risk of his life when he saved you from the power of Midian; [18]but you have risen against his family this day and have killed his seventy sons upon one stone, and have made Abimelech, the son of his handmaid, king over the citizens of Shechem, because he is your kinsman—[19]if, then, you have acted in good faith and with honor toward Jerubbaal and his family this day, rejoice in Abimelech and may he in turn rejoice in you. [20]But if not, let fire come forth from Abimelech to devour the citizens of Shechem and Beth-millo, and let fire come forth from the citizens and from Beth-millo to devour Abimelech." [21]Then Jotham went in flight to Beer, where he remained for fear of his brother Abimelech.

[22]When Abimelech had ruled Israel for three years, [23]God put bad feelings between Abimelech and the citizens of Shechem, who rebelled against Abimelech. [24]This was to repay the violence done to the seventy sons of Jerubbaal and to avenge their blood upon their brother Abimelech, who killed them, and upon the citizens of Shechem, who encouraged him to kill his brothers. [25]The citizens of Shechem then set men in ambush for him on the mountaintops, and these robbed all who passed them on the road. But it was reported to Abimelech.

[26]Now Gaal, son of Ebed, came over to Shechem with his kinsmen. The citizens of Shechem put their trust in him, [27]and went out into the fields, harvested their grapes and trod them out. Then they held a festival and went to the temple of their god, where they ate and drank and cursed Abimelech. [28]Gaal, son of Ebed, said, "Who is Abimelech? And why should we of Shechem serve him? Were not the son of Jerubbaal and his lieutenant Zebul once subject to the men of Hamor, father of Shechem? Why should we serve him? [29]Would that this people were entrusted to my command! I would depose Abimelech. I would say to Abimelech, 'Get a larger army and come out!' "

[30]At the news of what Gaal, son of Ebed, had said, Zebul, the ruler of the city, was angry [31]and sent messengers to Abimelech in Arumah with the information: "Gaal, son of Ebed, and his kinsmen have come to Shechem and are stirring up the city against you. [32]Now rouse yourself; set an ambush tonight in the fields, you and the men who are with you. [33]Promptly at sunrise tomorrow morning, make a raid on the city. When he and his followers come out against you, deal with him as best you can."

[34]During the night Abimelech advanced with all his soldiers and set up an ambush for Shechem in four companies. [35]Gaal, son of Ebed, went out and stood at the entrance of the city gate. When Abimelech and his soldiers rose from their

---

After only three years the citizens of Shechem rebel against Abimelech. The author attributes this to the action of God (v. 23) so as to bring on the succession of events that lead to the destruction of Shechem and the death of Abimelech. The civic assembly could depose the king as well as appoint him. What really brings things to a head is the arrival of Gaal, who instigates a full-scale rebellion against Abimelech (vv. 26-29).

When Abimelech hears of these matters from the ruler of the city, he arrives with his army and defeats Gaal (vv. 30-41). Notice that Abimelech does

place of ambush, ³⁶Gaal saw them and said to Zebul, "There are men coming down from the hilltops!" But Zebul answered him, "You see the shadow of the hills as men." ³⁷But Gaal went on to say, "Men are coming down from the region of Tabbur-Haares, and one company is coming by way of Elon-Meonenim." ³⁸Zebul said to him, "Where now is the boast you uttered, 'Who is Abimelech that we should serve him?' Are these not the men for whom you expressed contempt? Go out now and fight with them." ³⁹So Gaal went out at the head of the citizens of Shechem and fought against Abimelech. ⁴⁰But Abimelech routed him, and he fled before him; and many fell slain right up to the entrance of the gate. ⁴¹Abimelech returned to Arumah, but Zebul drove Gaal and his kinsmen from Shechem, which they had occupied.

⁴²The next day, when the people were taking the field, it was reported to Abimelech, ⁴³who divided the men he had into three companies, and set up an ambush in the fields. He watched till he saw the people leave the city, and then rose against them for the attack. ⁴⁴Abimelech and the company with him dashed in and stood by the entrance of the city gate, while the other two companies rushed upon all who were in the field and attacked them. ⁴⁵That entire day Abimelech fought against the city, and captured it. He then killed its inhabitants and demolished the city, sowing the site with salt.

⁴⁶When they heard of this, all the citizens of Migdal-shechem went into the crypt of the temple of El-berith. ⁴⁷It was reported to Abimelech that all the citizens of Migdal-shechem were gathered together. ⁴⁸So he went up Mount Zalmon with all his soldiers, took his ax in his hand, and cut down some brushwood. This he lifted to his shoulder, then said to the men with him, "Hurry! Do just as you have seen me do." ⁴⁹So all the men likewise cut down brushwood, and following Abimelech, placed it against the crypt. Then they set the crypt on fire over their heads, so that every one of the citizens of Migdal-shechem, about a thousand men and women, perished.

⁵⁰Abimelech proceeded to Thebez, which he invested and captured. ⁵¹Now there was a strong tower in the middle of

not live in Shechem but at Arumah, a town nearby. Tabbur-Haares means "navel of the world" and Elon-Meonenim means "diviner's oak." They refer to places near Shechem. Once Gaal is defeated Zebul will not allow him to continue to use Shechem as his base of operations, and Gaal disappears. The next day Abimelech returns and ambushes the people of Shechem as they come out to investigate the damage to their crops. Sowing a site with salt (v. 45) is an ancient rite of cursing. From verses 46-49 we learn that Abimelech has destroyed only the lower part of the city. The upper city stood on an artificial platform of earth that supported the ruler's palace and the temple of Baal Berith (also known as Beth-millo; see verses 6 and 20). The remaining citizens take refuge in the "crypt" of the temple of El-Berith. The true meaning of the Hebrew word translated "crypt" here is unknown. Some would translate it by "citadel." The reference is to some part of the fortified temple that Abimelech sets on fire, killing those who had taken refuge there (vv. 46-49).

the city, and all the men and women, in a word all the citizens of the city, fled there, shutting themselves in and going up to the roof of the tower. ⁵²Abimelech came up to the tower and fought against it, advancing to the very entrance of the tower to set it on fire. ⁵³But a certain woman cast the upper part of a millstone down on Abimelech's head, and it fractured his skull. ⁵⁴He immediately called his armor-bearer and said to him, "Draw your sword and dispatch me, lest they say of me that a woman killed me." So his attendant ran him through and he died. ⁵⁵When the Israelites saw that Abimelech was dead, they all left for their homes.

⁵⁶Thus did God requite the evil Abimelech had done to his father in killing his seventy brothers. ⁵⁷God also brought all their wickedness home to the Shechemites, for the curse of Jotham, son of Jerubbaal, overtook them.

10 Tola. ¹After Abimelech there rose to save Israel the Issacharite Tola,

son of Puah, son of Dodo, a resident of Shamir in the mountain region of Ephraim. ²When he had judged Israel twenty-three years, he died and was buried in Shamir.

Jair. ³Jair the Gileadite came after him and judged Israel twenty-two years. ⁴He had thirty sons who rode on thirty saddle-asses and possessed thirty cities in the land of Gilead; these are called Havvoth-jair to the present day. ⁵Jair died and was buried in Kamon.

Oppression by the Ammonites. ⁶The Israelites again offended the LORD, serving the Baals and Ashtaroths, the gods of Aram, the gods Sidon, the gods of Moab, the gods of the Ammonites, and the gods of the Philistines. Since they had abandoned the LORD and would not serve him, ⁷the LORD became angry with Israel and allowed them to fall into the power of [the Philistines and] the Ammonites. ⁸For eighteen years they afflicted and oppressed the Israelites in Bashan, and all the Israelites

Abimelech's end comes when he attacks Thebez, a town northeast of Shechem (vv. 50-55). Seemingly, Thebez had taken part in the revolt. Death at the hand of a woman was considered a disgrace (v. 54). With his death the first attempt at initiating the monarchy in Israel fails.

10:1-5 Tola and Jair. These are the first of the minor judges. There is a regular pattern followed in the descriptions of these men: name, origin, length of time in office, death, burial, and family. Since the numbers of years of their time in office are not stereotyped, they are probably original to the tradition. Though now they are said to have judged all Israel, their original sphere of influence was probably limited to a particular area. Also, their terms may have been contemporary with other minor judges or even one of the major judges. Their role is unclear. We have already explained in the introduction to this book that the Hebrew word meaning "to judge" can also mean "to rule." It is possible, then, that they were a type of local administrator. Tola is said to have "saved" Israel, perhaps meaning that after the confusion and unrest of the time of Abimelech, Tola brought some stability through his administration.

10:6–12:7 Jephthah. The story of Jephthah is a composite of various traditions to which some later additions have been made. The story proceeds

in the Amorite land beyond the Jordan in Gilead. ⁹The Ammonites also crossed the Jordan to fight against Judah, Benjamin, and the house of Ephraim, so that Israel was in great distress.

¹⁰Then the Israelites cried out to the LORD, "We have sinned against you; we have forsaken our God and have served the Baals." ¹¹The LORD answered the Israelites: "Did not the Egyptians, the Amorites, the Ammonites, the Philistines, ¹²the Sidonians, the Amalekites, and the Midianites oppress you? Yet when you cried out to me, and I saved you from their grasp, ¹³you still forsook me and worshiped other gods. Therefore I will save you no more. ¹⁴Go and cry out to the gods you have chosen; let them save

you now that you are in distress." ¹⁵But the Israelites said to the LORD, "We have sinned. Do to us whatever you please. Only save us this day." ¹⁶And they cast out the foreign gods from their midst and served the LORD, so that he grieved over the misery of Israel.

¹⁷The Ammonites had gathered for war and encamped in Gilead, while the Israelites assembled and encamped in Mizpah. ¹⁸And among the people the princes of Gilead said to one another, "The one who begins the war against the Ammonites shall be leader of all the inhabitants of Gilead."

11 **Jephthah.** ¹There was a chieftain, the Gileadite Jephthah, born to Gilead of a harlot. ²Gilead's wife had also

as follows: a prologue (10:6-16); the recall of Jephthah (10:17–11:11); Jephthah's negotiations with the Ammonites (11:12-28); Jephthah's vow and defeat of the Ammonites (11:29-40); and the defeat of the Ephraimites (12:1-7).

10:6-16 Prologue. These verses introduce the story of Jephthah and contain an expanded version of the D framework. What is interesting here is how this framework has been expanded: first by inserting the list of deities in verse 6; then the list of Israel's opponents, past, present, and future in verses 11 and 12; and the discussion between Yahweh and the people regarding Yahweh's response to their cry in verses 10-16. By recapitulating 2:6–3:6 and referring to the past and future enemies (Philistines) of Israel, this section becomes a theological introduction to the second half of the Book of Judges. The point is that there is nothing automatic about Yahweh's response to Israel's cry (see vv. 11-14). More than words admitting guilt are necessary. What eventually moves the Lord to grieve over the misery of the Israelites (v. 16) is that aside from admitting their guilt they also show themselves ready to accept punishment (v. 15) and, most importantly, to cast out the foreign gods from their midst (v. 16). The author is telling the exiles what is expected of them.

The oppressors this time are the Ammonites, who occupied the territory of the Moabites east of the Jordan River. They especially afflicted the Israelites in Bashan, east of the Jordan near the Sea of Galilee, and in the southern part of Gilead, which belonged to the tribe of Gad. At times they crossed over the Jordan and harried the southern tribes of Judah, Benjamin, and Ephraim.

borne him sons, and on growing up the sons of the wife had driven Jephthah away, saying to him, "You shall inherit nothing in our family, for you are the son of another woman." ³So Jephthah had fled from his brothers and had taken up residence in the land of Tob. A rabble had joined company with him, and went out with him on raids.

⁴Some time later, the Ammonites warred on Israel. ⁵When this occurred the elders of Gilead went to bring Jephthah from the land of Tob. ⁶"Come," they said to Jephthah, "be our commander that we may be able to fight the Ammonites." ⁷"Are you not the ones who hated me and drove me from my father's house?" Jephthah replied to the elders of Gilead. "Why do you come to me now, when you are in distress?" ⁸The elders of Gilead said to Jephthah, "In any case, we have now come back to you; if you go with us to fight against the Ammonites, you shall be the leader of all of us who dwell in Gilead." ⁹Jephthah answered the elders of Gilead, "If you bring me back to fight against the Ammonites and the LORD delivers them up to me, I shall be your leader." ¹⁰The elders of Gilead said to Jephthah, "The LORD is witness between us that we will do as you say."

¹¹So Jephthah went with the elders of Gilead, and the people made him their leader and commander. In Mizpah, Jephthah settled all his affairs before the LORD. ¹²Then he sent messengers to the king of the Ammonites to say, "What have you against me that you come to fight with me in my land?" ¹³He answered the messengers of Jephthah, "Israel took away my land from the Arnon to the Jabbok and the Jordan when they came up from Egypt. Now restore the same peaceably."

¹⁴Again Jephthah sent messengers to the king of the Ammonites, ¹⁵saying to him, "This is what Jephthah says: Israel did not take the land of Moab or the land of the Ammonites. ¹⁶For when they came up from Egypt, Israel went through the desert to the Red Sea and came to Kadesh. ¹⁷Israel then sent messengers to the king

10:17–11:1 Recall of Jephthah. It is obvious from 10:17-18 that none of the princes of Gilead wanted to begin the war against the Ammonites. Hence, attention turns to Jephthah, the chieftain of a group of brigands who plundered the area (vv. 1-3). Because of his illegitimate birth he had been driven out from his own land by the same people who now want him back to lead them in battle. Unlike the stories of the other judges, Jephthah's calling to be a judge does not take place in a single moment; rather, it takes place through negotiation. In negotiations with the elders (vv. 4-10) the elders first offer him only the role of commander (v. 6). When Jephthah does not immediately accept, they raise the ante to being "leader of all of us who dwell in Gilead" (v. 8). This seems to imply that the office of judge included administrative as well as military responsibilities. Verse 11 is about a certain form of investiture.

11:12-28 Negotiations with the Ammonites. Before rushing into battle Jephthah attempts to clarify the reasons for the Ammonite hostility and discovers that the Ammonites want back the land that they claim Israel took from them when they came up from Egypt (vv. 11-13). Jephthah then gives historical and theological justification for Israel's occupation of the disputed

of Edom saying, 'Let me pass through your land.' But the king of Edom did not give consent. They also sent to the king of Moab, but he too was unwilling. So Israel remained in Kadesh. ¹⁸Then they went through the desert, and by-passing the land of Edom and the land of Moab, went east of the land of Moab and encamped across the Arnon. Thus they did not go through the territory of Moab, for the Arnon is the boundary of Moab. ¹⁹Then Israel sent messengers to Sihon, king of the Amorites, king of Heshbon. Israel said to him, 'Let me pass through your land to my own place.' ²⁰But Sihon refused to let Israel pass through his territory. On the contrary, he gathered all his soldiers, who encamped at Jahaz and fought Israel. ²¹But the LORD, the God of Israel, delivered Sihon and all his men into the power of Israel, who defeated them and occupied all the land of the Amorites dwelling in that region, ²²the whole territory from the Arnon to the Jabbok, from the desert to the Jordan. ²³If now the LORD, the God of Israel, has cleared the Amorites out of the way of his people, are you to dislodge Israel? ²⁴Should you not possess that which your god Chemosh gave you to possess, and should we not possess all that the LORD, our God, has cleared out for us? ²⁵Again, are you any better than Balak, son of Zippor, king of Moab? Did he ever quarrel with Israel, or did he war against them ²⁶when Israel occupied Heshbon and its villages, Aroer and its villages, and all the cities on the banks of the Arnon? Three hundred years have passed; why did you not recover them during that time? ²⁷I have not sinned against you, but you wrong me by warring against me. Let the LORD, who is judge, decide this day between the Israelites and the Ammonites!" ²⁸But the king of the Ammonites paid no heed to the message Jephthah sent him.

Jephthah's Vow. ²⁹The spirit of the LORD came upon Jephthah. He passed through Gilead and Manasseh, and through Mizpah-Gilead as well, and from there he went on to the Ammonites. ³⁰Jephthah made a vow to the LORD. "If

land east of the Jordan. The material in verses 13-27 is no doubt a later insertion to justify Israel's possession of the land between the Arnon and Jabbok rivers. The historical argument is that the territory in dispute did not belong to either Ammon or Moab but was part of the former kingdom of Sihon, which Israel had conquered under Moses. The theological argument is that territories belong to those who received them from their particular deity and the Israelite God had given them this territory. The historical survey in verses 15-22 is in basic agreement with Num 20–24.

11:29-40 Jephthah's vow and defeat of the Ammonites. The spirit of the Lord now comes upon Jephthah and he inflicts a severe defeat upon the Ammonites. The center of attention in this scene is Jephthah's vow that if the Lord will deliver the Ammonites into his power, he will offer up to the Lord as a holocaust whoever comes out of his house upon his return (vv. 30-31). The one who comes out is his daughter. There are a number of parallels to this event in comparative folklore. The surprising thing is that the author has not censored this report of human sacrifice! Elsewhere in the Old Testament it is condemned (Lev 18:21; 20:2-5; Deut 12:31; 18:10; Mic 6:7). The fact of human sacrifice here is secondary, however, to the theme

you deliver the Ammonites into my power," he said, [31]"whoever comes out of the doors of my house to meet me when I return in triumph from the Ammonites shall belong to the LORD. I shall offer him up as a holocaust."

[32]Jephthah then went on to the Ammonites to fight against them, and the LORD delivered them into his power, [33]so that he inflicted a severe defeat on them, from Aroer to the approach of Minnith (twenty cities in all) and as far as Abel-keramim. Thus were the Ammonites brought into subjection by the Israelites. [34]When Jephthah returned to his house in Mizpah, it was his daughter who came forth, playing the tambourines and dancing. She was an only child: he had neither son nor daughter besides her. [35]When he saw her, he rent his garments and said, "Alas, daughter, you have struck me down and brought calamity upon me. For I have made a vow to the LORD and I cannot retract." [36]"Father," she replied, "you have made a vow to the LORD. Do with me as you have vowed, because the LORD has wrought vengeance for you on your enemies the Ammonites." [37]Then she said to her father, "Let me have this favor. Spare me for two

months, that I may go off down the mountains to mourn my virginity with my companions." [38]"Go," he replied, and sent her away for two months. So she departed with her companions and mourned her virginity on the mountains. [39]At the end of the two months she returned to her father, who did to her as he had vowed. She had not been intimate with man. It then became a custom in Israel [40]for Israelite women to go yearly to mourn the daughter of Jephthah the Gileadite for four days of the year.

12 **The Shibboleth Incident.** [1]The men of Ephraim gathered together and crossed over to Zaphon. They said to Jephthah, "Why do you go on to fight with the Ammonites without calling us to go with you? We will burn your house over you." [2]Jephthah answered them, "My soldiers and I were engaged in a critical contest with the Ammonites. I summoned you, but you did not rescue me from their power. [3]When I saw that you would not effect a rescue, I took my life in my own hand and went on to the Ammonites, and the LORD delivered them into my power. Why, then, do you come up against me this day to fight with me?"

of the irrevocability of Jephthah's vow. The vow, once it has been made, must be kept. What complicates the situation is that the story is now used as an etiology for a defunct lamentation festival in Israel (vv. 39-40). Some see the story as a myth passed off as history to explain the festival. Perhaps the story is meant to show the lamentable effects of not trusting in the Lord's willingness to save Israel. There is no need for such pagan practices.

12:1-7 Defeat of the Ephraimites. This story, which preserves memories of frontier conflicts between Gilead and Ephraim, is loosely joined to the rest. As in the story of Gideon (8:1ff.) the Ephraimites are upset because they had not been summoned to help in the battle against the Ammonites. Jephthah claims that they had been invited but had not responded (vv. 1-3). In the dialect spoken by the Ephraimites the initial sibilant of "Shibboleth" could not be pronounced correctly, thus giving them away. The meaning of the taunt in verse 4 is not clear.

⁴Then Jephthah called together all the men of Gilead and fought against Ephraim, whom they defeated; for the Ephraimites had said, "You of Gilead are Ephraimite fugitives in territory belonging to Ephraim and Manasseh." ⁵The Gileadites took the fords of the Jordan toward Ephraim. When any of the fleeing Ephraimites said, "Let me pass," the men of Gilead would say to him, "Are you an Ephraimite?" If he answered, "No!" ⁶they would ask him to say "Shibboleth." If he said "Sibboleth," not being able to give the proper pronunciation, they would seize him and kill him at the fords of the Jordan. Thus forty-two thousand Ephraimites fell at that time.

⁷After having judged Israel for six years, Jephthah the Gileadite died and was buried in his city in Gilead.

Ibzan. ⁸After him Ibzan of Bethlehem judged Israel. ⁹He had thirty sons. He also had thirty daughters married outside the family, and he brought in as wives for his sons thirty young women from outside the family. After having judged Israel for seven years, ¹⁰Ibzan died and was buried in Bethlehem.

Elon. ¹¹After him the Zebulunite Elon judged Israel. When he had judged Israel for ten years, ¹²the Zebulunite Elon died and was buried in Elon in the land of Zebulun.

Abdon. ¹³After him the Pirathonite Abdon, son of Hillel, judged Israel. ¹⁴He had forty sons and thirty grandsons who rode on seventy saddle-asses. After having judged Israel for eight years, ¹⁵the Pirathonite Abdon, son of Hillel, died and was buried in Pirathon in the land of Ephraim on the mountain of the Amalekites.

13 **The Birth of Samson.** ¹The Israelites again offended the

The conclusion to the story of Jephthah in 12:7 is from the formula used for the minor judges, leading some to see Jephthah as a later development of one who was originally only one of the minor judges. This idea is supported by the fact that the story of Jephthah stands between the two lists of the minor judges (10:1-5 and 12:8-15).

12:8-15 Ibzan, Elon and Abdon. This is the second and final list of the minor judges, following the pattern of the first list (10:1-5).

13:1–16:31 Samson. The Samson stories contain the most extensive cycle of traditions in the Book of Judges. Though there is no reason to deny their historicity, it is clear that these traditions have been deeply colored by legendary, cultic, and folklore elements—possibly even by ancient solar myths. Samson's name is related to the Hebrew word for sun, and he comes from an area not far from Beth-shemesh (temple of the sun).

There are some significant differences between the Samson traditions and the other material in the book. The D framework is reduced to a report on the sin of the people and the Lord's deliverance of them into the power of the Philistines. Nothing is said of a cry to the Lord. Also, Samson never commands an army and he does not liberate Israel either from the Philistines or from any other oppressor. His relations with the Philistines appear to be on the level of a private feud. However, the editor sees these exploits as the beginning of Israel's deliverance from the power of the Philistines.

LORD, who therefore delivered them into the power of the Philistines for forty years.

²There was a certain man from Zorah, of the clan of the Danites, whose name was Manoah. His wife was barren and had borne no children. ³An angel of the LORD appeared to the woman and said to her, "Though you are barren and have had no children, yet you will conceive and bear a son. ⁴Now, then, be careful to take no wine or strong drink and to eat nothing unclean. ⁵As for the son you will conceive and bear, no razor shall touch his head, for this boy is to be consecrated to God from the womb. It is he who will begin the deliverance of Israel from the power of the Philistines."

⁶The woman went and told her husband, "A man of God came to me; he had the appearance of an angel of God, terrible indeed. I did not ask him where he

Each of the various traditions had its own prior independent existence. However, the editor has artfully woven them together into a coherent whole. The material falls into four sections: the birth of Samson (ch. 13); the marriage of Samson (ch. 14); Samson's defeat of the Philistines (ch. 15); and the capture and death of Samson (ch. 16).

13:1-25 The birth of Samson. The chapter begins with a short form of the D framework (v. 1). The Philistines had entered Palestine about fifty years after the Israelites as part of the migration of the sea peoples from the Aegean and Crete. Repulsed by the Egyptians around 1200 B.C., they had settled on the southern coast of Palestine.

Verses 2-5 report the angel's announcement of the forthcoming birth of Samson to his unnamed mother. His father is from Zorah, a town in the territory originally allotted to the tribe of Dan and the point of departure for the migration of the Danites to the extreme northern part of Palestine (ch. 18). Barrenness is a common theme in the Old Testament (see Gen 11:30 and 1 Sam 1:2f.) and is used as an occasion for a miraculous divine intervention whereby a child is born to undertake a unique mission. In verses 4 and 5 the nazirite rule (Num 6:1-8) is adapted for the consecration of a person in the womb. Normally nazirites were adults who voluntarily consecrated themselves to the Lord for life or for a particular period. Samson is consecrated from his conception, so the rites before his birth apply also to his mother. The regulations that Samson will live under are: abstaining from wine and strong drink, not shaving his head, and avoiding all contact with the dead. Verse 7 adds that he will be a nazirite until his death.

Because the following chapters do not refer to the nazirite vow that Samson is under, it is possible that this chapter was composed as the introduction to the cycle later on in order to make the story of Samson a narrative of the violation of the nazirite vow. It is this sinful person whom the Lord uses to begin the deliverance of the people from the power of the Philistines (v. 5).

came from, nor did he tell me his name. ⁷But he said to me, 'You will be with child and will bear a son. So take neither wine nor strong drink, and eat nothing unclean. For the boy shall be consecrated to God from the womb, until the day of his death.' " ⁸Manoah then prayed to the LORD. "O LORD, I beseech you," he said, "may the man of God whom you sent, return to us to teach us what to do for the boy who will be born."

⁹God heard the prayer of Manoah, and the angel of God came again to the woman as she was sitting in the field. Since her husband Manoah was not with her, ¹⁰the woman ran in haste and told her husband. "The man who came to me the other day has appeared to me," she said to him; ¹¹so Manoah got up and followed his wife. When he reached the man, he said to him, "Are you the one who spoke to my wife?" "Yes," he answered. ¹²Then Manoah asked, "Now, when that which you say comes true, what are we expected to do for the boy?" ¹³The angel of the LORD answered Manoah, "Your wife it to abstain from all the things of which I spoke to her. ¹⁴She must not eat anything that comes from the vine, nor take wine or strong drink, nor eat anything unclean. Let her observe all that I have commanded her." ¹⁵Then Manoah said to the angel of the LORD, "Can we persuade you to stay, while we prepare a kid for you?" ¹⁶But the angel of the LORD answered Manoah,

"Although you press me, I will not partake of your food. But if you will, you may offer a holocaust to the LORD." Not knowing that it was the angel of the LORD, ¹⁷Manoah said to him, "What is your name, that we may honor you when your words come true?" ¹⁸The angel of the LORD answered him, "Why do you ask my name, which is mysterious?" ¹⁹Then Manoah took the kid with a cereal offering and offered it on the rock to the LORD, whose works are mysteries. While Manoah and his wife were looking on, ²⁰as the flame rose to the sky from the altar, the angel of the LORD ascended in the flame of the altar. When Manoah and his wife saw this, they fell prostrate to the ground; ²¹but the angel of the LORD was seen no more by Manoah and his wife. Then Manoah, realizing that it was the angel of the LORD, ²²said to his wife, "We will certainly die, for we have seen God." ²³But his wife pointed out to him, "If the LORD had meant to kill us, he would not have accepted a holocaust and cereal offering from our hands! Nor would he have let us see all this just now, or hear what we have heard."

²⁴The woman bore a son and named him Samson. The boy grew up and the LORD blessed him; ²⁵the spirit of the LORD first stirred him in Mahaneh-dan, which is between Zorah and Eshtaol.

14 **Marriage of Samson.** ¹Samson went down to Timnah and saw there one of the Philistine women. ²On

In verses 6-23 Samson's father, Manoah, shows typical Semitic caution about the testimony of a woman and so needs to hear for himself what he and his wife must do for the boy who will be born (vv. 8-14). Manoah, in his conversation with the angel, is looking for a sign, which he receives in the consumption of the holocaust by fire and the ascent of the angel in the flame (v. 19). Only then is he convinced that the messenger is from God. When Manoah asks his name, the angel does not reveal it, saying that it is "mysterious," i.e., incomprehensible, like the works of God (see vv. 18 and 19).

his return he told his father and mother, "There is a Philistine woman I saw in Timnah whom I wish you to get as a wife for me." ³His father and mother said to him, "Can you find no wife among your kinsfolk or among all our people, that you must go and take a wife from the uncircumcised Philistines?" But Samson answered his father, "Get her for me, for she pleases me." ⁴Now his father and mother did not know that this had been brought about by the LORD, who was providing an opportunity against the Philistines; for at that time they had dominion over Israel.

⁵So Samson went down to Timnah with his father and mother. When they had come to the vineyards of Timnah, a young lion came roaring to meet him. ⁶But the spirit of the LORD came upon Samson, and although he had no weapons, he tore the lion in pieces as one tears a kid. ⁷However, on the journey to speak for the woman, he did not mention to his father or mother what he had done. ⁸Later, when he returned to marry the woman who pleased him, he stepped aside to look at the remains of the lion and found a swarm of bees and honey in the lion's carcass. ⁹So he scooped the honey out into his palms and ate it as he went along. When he came to his father and mother, he gave them some to eat, without telling them that he had scooped the honey from the lion's carcass.

¹⁰His father also went down to the woman, and Samson gave a banquet there, since it was customary for the young men to do this. ¹¹When they met him, they brought thirty men to be his

14:1-20 The marriage of Samson. Samson's first exploits take place in the context of his marriage. At Timnah, a Philistine town a few miles from Zorah, Samson falls in love with a Philistine woman and asks his parents to obtain her for his bride (vv. 1-3). Normally, marriage negotiations were carried out by the bridegroom's father. Samson's parents are displeased because she is not an Israelite; a foreign wife was considered dangerous to security. "Uncircumcised" (v. 3) is used only of the Philistines in the Old Testament, pointing to the fact that they were the only ones in the region who did not practice the rite of circumcision. Perhaps the editor did not approve of this marriage either, but in verse 4 he provides the interpretative key for the rest of the chapter: what is about to take place is part of God's plan. Though not explicit, it appears that the editor sees the events here, especially those in verses 19-20, as the way the Lord begins the deliverance of Israel from the Philistines (13:5).

The whole process of Samson's coming and going to Timnah (vv. 5-9, 10) is obscure, and the references to his parents in verses 5 and 10 are awkward. These references might be later additions to show that Samson's parents went along with him and set up the marriage in spite of their opposition. The important issue, however, is the killing of the lion and later finding the honey in its carcass. It is the spirit of the Lord that gives Samson the strength to deal so easily with the lion (v. 6). Notice that Samson breaks the nazirite vow by eating the honey, which is impure because it has been taken from a corpse.

companions. ¹²Samson said to them, "Let me propose a riddle to you. If within the seven days of the feast you solve it for me successfully, I will give you thirty linen tunics and thirty sets of garments. ¹³But if you cannot answer it for me, you must give me thirty tunics and thirty sets of garments." "Propose your riddle," they responded; "we will listen to it." ¹⁴So he said to them,

"Out of the eater came forth food,
    and out of the strong came forth
    sweetness."

After three days' failure to answer the riddle, ¹⁵they said on the fourth day to Samson's wife, "Coax your husband to answer the riddle for us, or we will burn you and your family. Did you invite us here to reduce us to poverty?" ¹⁶At Samson's side, his wife wept and said, "You must hate me; you do not love me, for you have proposed a riddle to my countrymen, but have not told me the answer." He said to her, "If I have not told it even to my father or my mother, must I tell it to you?" ¹⁷But she wept beside him during the seven days the feast lasted. On the seventh day, since she importuned him, he told her the answer, and she explained the riddle to her countrymen.

¹⁸On the seventh day, before the sun set, the men of the city said to him,

"What is sweeter than honey,
    and what is stronger than a lion?"

He replied to them,

"If you had not plowed with my heifer,
    you would not have solved my riddle."

¹⁹The spirit of the LORD came upon him, and he went down to the Ashkelon, where he killed thirty of their men and despoiled them; he gave their garments to those who had answered the riddle. Then he went off to his own family in anger, ²⁰and Samson's wife was married to the one who had been best man at his wedding.

15 **Samson Defeats the Philistines.** ¹After some time, in the season of the wheat harvest, Samson visited his wife, bringing a kid. But when he said, "Let me be with my wife in private," her father would not let him enter, ²saying, "I thought it certain you wished to repudiate her; so I gave her to your best man. Her younger sister is more beautiful than she; you may have her in-

Samson's riddle (vv. 10-18) is impossible to solve unless one knows about the private actions of the hero. The Philistines are able to answer it only by threatening his new wife (v. 15). This treachery causes Samson to perform one of his feats against the Philistines (v. 19). Ashkelon was a Philistine stronghold on the coast, southwest of Timnah.

15:1-20 Defeat of the Philistines. After his anger subsides Samson goes to visit his wife, taking along the gift of a kid (v. 1). However, he is refused entrance to visit her because her father has already given her to Samson's best man, having interpreted Samson's abrupt withdrawal (14:19) as a repudiation and divorce of her. The father proposes an alternative, but Samson departs in anger (v. 3).

The incident with the foxes is difficult to visualize (vv. 4-5). It is obviously intended to be some sort of guerilla tactic. In all of this Samson seems to be overreacting, since he had been offended by only one family.

stead." ³Samson said to them, "This time the Philistines cannot blame me if I harm them." ⁴So Samson left and caught three hundred foxes. Turning them tail to tail, he tied between each pair of tails one of the torches he had at hand. ⁵He then kindled the torches and set the foxes loose in the standing grain of the Philistines, thus burning both the shocks and the standing grain, and the vineyards and olive orchards as well.

⁶When the Philistines asked who had done this, they were told, "Samson, the son-in-law of the Timnite, because his wife was taken and given to his best man." So the Philistines went up and destroyed her and her family by fire. ⁷Samson said to them, "If this is how you act, I will not stop until I have taken revenge on you." ⁸And with repeated blows, he inflicted a great slaughter on them. Then he went down and remained in a cavern of the cliff of Etam.

⁹The Philistines went up and, from a camp in Judah, deployed against Lehi. ¹⁰When the men of Judah asked, "Why have you come up against us?" they answered, "To take Samson prisoner; to do to him as he has done to us." ¹¹Three thousand men of Judah went down to the cavern in the cliff of Etam and said to Samson, "Do you not know that the Philistines are our rulers? Why, then,

have you done this to us?" He answered them, "As they have done to me, so have I done to them," ¹²They said to him, "We have come to take you prisoner, to deliver you over to the Philistines." Samson said to them, "Swear to me that you will not kill me yourselves." ¹³"No," they replied, "we will certainly not kill you but will only bind you and deliver you over to them." So they bound him with two new ropes and brought him up from the cliff. ¹⁴When he reached Lehi, and the Philistines came shouting to meet him, the spirit of the LORD came upon him: the ropes around his arms became as flax that is consumed by fire and his bonds melted away from his hands. ¹⁵Near him was the fresh jawbone of an ass; he reached out, grasped it, and with it killed a thousand men. ¹⁶Then Samson said,

"With the jawbone of an ass
   I have piled them in a heap;
With the jawbone of an ass
   I have slain a thousand men."

¹⁷As he finished speaking he threw the jawbone from him; and so that place was named Ramath-lehi. ¹⁸Being very thirsty, he cried to the LORD and said, "You have granted this great victory by the hand of your servant. Must I now die of thirst or fall into the hands of the uncircumcised?" ¹⁹Then God split the cavity in Lehi, and water issued from it, which Samson

---

The Philistines retaliate swiftly against Samson's wife and her family, and Samson takes revenge against the Philistines (vv. 6-8). Having escaped to Etam in the territory of the tribe of Judah, the Philistines pressure Judah to turn Samson over to them (vv. 9-10). The sites of both Etam and Lehi are unknown. Lehi means "jawbone," its presence here preparing us for the word-play in verse 17. Men of Judah now go down to capture Samson and, to their surprise, find him ready to surrender (vv. 11-13). That they did not expect such an easy time is reflected in the large number who set out for him (v. 11). When Samson sees the Philistines the spirit of the Lord comes upon him, moving him once again to extraordinary action (vv. 14-16), another deed by which the Lord begins to deliver Israel from the Philistines (see 13:5).

drank till his spirit returned and he-revived. Hence that spring in Lehi iscalled En-hakkore to this day.

²⁰Samson judged Israel for twenty years in the days of the Philistines.

16 ¹Once Samson went to Gaza, where he saw a harlot and visited her. ²Informed that Samson had come there, the men of Gaza surrounded him with an ambush at the city gate all night long. And all the night they waited, saying, "Tomorrow morning we will kill him." ³Samson rested there until midnight. Then he rose, seized the doors of the city gate and the two gateposts, and tore them loose, bar and all. He hoisted them on his shoulders and carried them to the top of the ridge opposite Hebron.

Samson and Delilah. ⁴After that he fell in love with a woman in the Wadi Sorek whose name was Delilah. ⁵The lords of the Philistines came to her and said, "Beguile him and find out the secret of his great strength, and how we may overcome and bind him so as to keep him helpless. We will each give you eleven hundred shekels of silver."

⁶So Delilah said to Samson, "Tell me the secret of your great strength and how you may be bound so as to be kept helpless." ⁷"If they bind me with seven fresh bowstrings which have not dried," Samson answered her, "I shall be as weak as any other man." ⁸So the lords of the Philistines brought her seven fresh bowstrings which had not dried, and she bound him with them. ⁹She had men lying in wait in the chamber and so she said to him, "The Philistines are upon you, Samson!" But he snapped the strings as a thread of tow is severed by a whiff of flame; and the secret of his strength remained unknown.

¹⁰Delilah said to Samson, "You have mocked me and told me lies. Now tell me how you may be bound." ¹¹If they bind me tight with new ropes, with which no work has been done," he answered her, "I shall be as weak as any other man." ¹²So Delilah took new ropes and bound him with them. Then she said to him, "The Philistines are upon you, Samson!" For there were men lying in wait in the chamber. But he snapped them off his arms like thread.

¹³Delilah said to Samson again, "Up to now you have mocked me and told me lies. Tell me how you may be bound." He said to her, "If you weave my seven locks of hair into the web and fasten them with the pin, I shall be as weak as any other man." ¹⁴So while he slept, Delilah wove his seven locks of hair into the web, and fastened them in with the pin. Then she said, "The Philistines are upon you, Samson!" Awakening from his sleep, he pulled out both the weaver's pin and the web.

¹⁵Then she said to him, "How can you say that you love me when you do not confide in me? Three times already you

Notice that Samson again violates the law of the nazirite by touching an animal carcass. Verse 17 tells us that the name of the site "Ramath-lehi" (throwing of the jawbone) is explained by Samson's action of discarding the weapon. Verses 18-19 present the etiology of a spring at Lehi called "Enhak-kore," that is, "spring of one who called."

The notice about Samson's judgeship in verse 20 probably indicates a conclusion to an early edition of the Samson stories and that chapter 16 was added later (see 16:31).

16:1-31 The capture and death of Samson. This chapter has three separate episodes: Samson and the harlot (vv. 1-3); Samson and Delilah

have mocked me, and not told me the secret of your great strength!" ¹⁶She importuned him continually and vexed him with her complaints till he was deathly weary of them. ¹⁷So he took her completely into his confidence and told her, "No razor has touched my head, for I have been consecrated to God from my mother's womb. If I am shaved, my strength will leave me, and I shall be as weak as any other man!" ¹⁸When Delilah saw that he had taken her completely into his confidence, she summoned the lords of the Philistines, saying, "Come up this time, for he has opened his heart to me." So the lords of the Philistines came and brought up the money with them. ¹⁹She had him sleep on her lap, and called for a man who shaved off his seven locks of hair. Then she began to mistreat him, for his strength had left him. ²⁰When she said, "The Philistines are upon you, Samson!", and he woke from his sleep, he thought he could make good his escape as he had done time and again, for he did not realize that the LORD had left him. ²¹But the Philistines seized him and gouged out his eyes. Then they brought him down to Gaza and bound him with bronze fetters, and he was put to grinding in the prison. ²²But the hair of his head began to grow as soon as it was shaved off.

(vv. 4-22); and the death of Samson (vv. 23-31). While the last two episodes are clearly related, the first one appears to be independent. However, because of its emphasis on Samson's strength, it is a good preparation for the question in verse 5.

The episode with the harlot (vv. 1-3) takes place at Gaza, one of the Philistine cities on the southern coast of Palestine. The city gates at that time had a tunnel-like opening that was flanked by guardrooms. Samson was able to escape the ambush at the gate by leaving at an unexpected time when the men were waiting in the guardrooms, since they did not expect Samson to leave until the morning. The distance from Gaza to Hebron is about 38 miles and uphill.

Samson now falls in love with Delilah. This episode (vv. 4-22) is a series of stereotyped scenes in which Samson is shown as so infatuated with Delilah that his behavior is ridiculous and abnormal. A strong element of magic runs through the episode. First of all, the Philistines appear to believe that some magical or supernatural force gives Samson his strength (v. 5). Samson's first three explanations of his strength are also based on magical ideas (vv. 6-14). Bowstrings (v. 7) were made from the tendons of slaughtered animals; hence, once again Samson disregards the nazirite rule by coming into contact with part of a corpse. Finally, the fourth time that Samson gives the explanation for his strength he tells the truth (vv. 15-17). This is the first time that Samson's strength is presented as something permanent and residing in his unshorn hair. In the other stories his strength is given only on specific occasions as a gift of the spirit of the Lord (14:6, 19; 15:14). The story in 16:1-3, however, presumes some kind of permanent strength, as does 15:8. The ominous note in verse 22 prepares for verses 28-30, where Samson's strength

The Death of Samson. [23]The lords of the Philistines assembled to offer a great sacrifice to their god Dagon and to make merry. They said,

"Our god has delivered into our power Samson our enemy."

[25]When their spirits were high, they said, "Call Samson that he may amuse us." So they called Samson from the prison, and he played the buffoon before them. [24]When the people saw him, they praised their god. For they said,

"Our god has delivered into our power
our enemy, the ravager of our land,
the one who has multiplied our slain."

Then they stationed him between the columns. [26]Samson said to the attendant who was holding his hand, "Put me where I may touch the columns that support the temple and may rest against them." [27]The temple was full of men and women: all the lords of the Philistines were there, and from the roof about three thousand men and women looked on as Samson provided amusement. [28]Samson cried out to the LORD and said, "O LORD God, remember me! Strengthen me, O God, this last time that for my two eyes I may avenge myself once and for all on the Philistines." [29]Samson grasped the two middle columns on which the temple

is again the result of a gift of the Lord. One can see the tension between the older stories about Samson's extraordinary strength and the later editor's theological explanation of his strength as a gift of the Lord for the deliverance of Israel. Samson is unable to escape after his hair has been cut off (v. 20) because the Lord has left him. The final breaking of the nazirite rule—once too often—occurs with the shaving of Samson's head.

Perhaps the reason that the death episode (vv. 23-31) was added was to show that though Samson had squandered away his strength out of his own self-interest, in the end he turned to the Lord (v. 28) and died honorably by bringing about God's justice on the Philistines. Dagon (v. 23) was an ancient agricultural deity of the West Semitic world. In the Bible he appears exclusively as a Philistine deity. Dagon means "grain." The number three thousand in verse 27 seems an exaggeration, and was probably the editor's intention in view of the statement in verse 30.

The chapter concludes (v. 31) by repeating the length of time that Samson judged Israel (see 15:20). No reference is made to any peace in the land, since the editor realized that Samson's exploits were only the beginning of the deliverance from the Philistines.

PART III: APPENDIX

Judg 17:1–21:25

The appendix to the Book of Judges contains two episodes that have been placed here because they deal with the period before the monarchy: the migration of Dan to the north (17:1–18:31); and the civil war against Benjamin (19:1–21:25).

rested and braced himself against them, one at his right hand, the other at his left. ³⁰And Samson said, "Let me die with the Philistines!" He pushed hard, and the temple fell upon the lords and all the people who were in it. Those he killed at his death were more than those he had killed during his lifetime.

³¹All his family and kinsmen went down and bore him up for burial in the grave of his father Manoah between Zorah and Eshtaol. He had judged Israel for twenty years.

III: THE TRIBES OF DAN AND BENJAMIN IN THE DAYS OF THE JUDGES

17 Micah and the Levite. ¹There was a man in the mountain region of Ephraim whose name was Micah. ²He said to his mother, "The eleven hundred shekels of silver over which you pronounced a curse in my hearing when they were taken from you, are in my possession. It was I who took them; so now I will restore them to you." ³When he restored the eleven hundred shekels of silver to his mother, she took two hundred of them and gave them to the silversmith, who made of them a carved idol overlaid with silver. ⁴Then his mother said, "May the LORD bless my son! I have consecrated the silver to the LORD as my gift in favor of my son, by making a carved idol overlaid with silver." It re-

mained in the house of Micah. ⁵Thus the layman Micah had a sanctuary. He also made an ephod and household idols, and consecrated one of his sons, who became his priest. ⁶In those days there was no king in Israel; everyone did what he thought best.

⁷There was a young Levite who had resided within the tribe of Judah at Bethlehem of Judah. ⁸From that city he set out to find another place of residence. On his journey he came to the house of Micah in the mountain region of Ephraim. ⁹Micah said to him, "Where do you come from?" He answered him, "I am a Levite from Bethlehem in Judah, and am on my way to find some other place of residence." ¹⁰"Stay with me," Micah said to him. "Be father and priest to me, and I will give you ten silver shekels a year, a set of garments, and your food." ¹¹So the young Levite decided to stay with the man, to whom he became as one of his own sons. ¹²Micah consecrated the young Levite, who became his priest, remaining in his house. ¹³Therefore Micah said, "Now I know that the LORD will prosper me, since the Levite has become my priest."

18 Migration of the Danites. ¹At that time there was no king in Israel. Moreover the tribe of Danites were in search of a district to dwell in, for up to that time they had received no heritage among the tribes of Israel.

The statement, "In those days there was no king in Israel; everyone did what he thought best," appears at the beginning (17:6) and at the end of the appendix (21:25). In both 18:1 and 19:1 there is the reminder that "at that time there was no king in Israel." These are really pro-monarchy statements that the editor has inserted because he did not see the events narrated in these chapters as commendable. They could only have happened because there was no king in the land. The editor saw the monarchy as a necessary stabilizing factor in Israel.

17:1–18:31 The migration of Dan. The purpose of these two chapters is not merely to report on the history of the tribe of Dan, but to give infor-

²So the Danites sent from their clan a detail of five valiant men of Zorah and Eshtaol, to reconnoiter the land and scout it. With their instructions to go and scout the land, they traveled as far as the house of Micah in the mountain region of Ephraim, where they passed the night. ³Near the house of Micah, theyrecognized the voice of the young Levite and turned in that direction. "Who brought you here and what are you doing here?" they asked him. "What is your interest here?" ⁴"This is how Micah treats me," he replied to them. "He pays me a salary and I am his priest." ⁵They said to him, "Consult God, that we may know whether the undertaking we are engaged in will succeed." ⁶The priest said to them, "Go and prosper: the Lord is favorable to the undertaking you are engaged in."

⁷So the five men went on and came to Laish. They saw that the people dwelling there lived securely after the manner of the Sidonians, quiet and trusting, with no lack of any natural resources. They were distant from the Sidonians and had no contact with other people. ⁸When the five returned to their kinsmen in Zorah and Eshtaol and were asked for a report, ⁹they replied, "Come, let us attack them, for we have seen the land and it is very good. Are you going to hesitate? Do not be slothful about beginning your expedition to possess the land. ¹⁰Those against whom you go are a trusting people, and the land is ample. God has indeed given it into your power: a place where no natural resource is lacking."

¹¹So six hundred men of the clan of the Danites, fully armed with weapons of war, set out from where they were in Zorah and Eshtaol, ¹²and camped in Judah, up near Kiriath-jearim; hence to this day the place, which lies west of Kiriath-jearim, is called Mahaneh-dan.

¹³From there they went on to the mountain region of Ephraim and came to the house of Micah. ¹⁴The five men who had gone to reconnoiter the land of Laish said to their kinsmen, "Do you know that in these houses there are an ephod, household idols, and a carved idol overlaid with silver? Now decide what you must do!" ¹⁵So turning in that direction, they went to the house of the young Levite at the home of Micah and greeted

mation about the origins and nature of the sanctuary of Dan. This sanctuary had become important in 922 B.C. when the northern tribes had broken off from the southern tribes and formed the kingdom of Israel. As a result of this break, the sanctuary at Dan had become the national sanctuary of the northern kingdom along with the sanctuary at Bethel. The priests in Jerusalem frowned upon the Yahweh cult at the sanctuary of Dan. These two chapters argue against this sanctuary by pointing out that its cult there represented a merger of disparate worshipers, and that the silver used for making the sacred object kept there derived from stolen money. The priesthood there, although having a noble lineage, is also shown as having been compromised.

Chapter 17 is a background for the events in chapter 18. Note that the carved idol (vv. 3-4) is an idol of Yahweh, something that is strictly forbidden by the Mosaic law (see Exod 20:4-6). Micah also makes an ephod (see 8:24-27) and household idols, i.e., items used for divining (v. 5). In the beginning he makes one of his sons the priest, i.e., one who took care of the sanctuary and gave oracles.

ιim. ¹⁶The six hundred men girt with weapons of war, who were Danites, stood by the entrance of the gate, and the priest tood there also. ¹⁷Meanwhile the five men who had gone to reconnoiter the and went up and entered the house of Micah. ¹⁸When they had gone in and taken the ephod, the household idols, and he carved idol overlaid with silver, the priest said to them, "What are you doing?" ¹⁹They said to him, "Be still: put your hand over your mouth. Come with us and be our father and priest. Is it better for you to be priest for the family of one man or to be priest for a tribe and a clan of Israel?" ²⁰The priest, agreeing, took the ephod, household idols, and carved idol and went off in the midst of the band. ²¹As they turned to depart, they placed their little ones, their livestock, and their goods at the head of the column.

²²The Danites had already gone some distance, when those in the houses near that of Micah took up arms and overtook them. ²³They called to the Danites, who turned about and said to Micah, "What do you want, that you have taken up arms?" ²⁴"You have taken my god, which I made, and have gone off with my priest as well," he answered. "What is left for

A young Levite from Bethlehem comes looking for a better situation, and Micah convinces him to be his priest (vv. 7-13). Micah's concern to have a Levite priest suggests that Levites were already known for being more skilled in cultic matters. The title "father" (v. 10) emphasizes the priest's role as cultic diviner and oracle giver.

Chapter 18 begins by stating that the Danites were searching for an area in which to live, since they had received no heritage among the tribes of Israel v. 1). This statement is difficult to accept in light of Josh 19:40-48. They had been allotted territory to the west of Benjamin and south of Ephraim and north of Judah. However, they were so restricted by the Amorites and Philistines (see 1:34) that they could not control their territory, so they sent out scouts to look for a better district. Zorah and Eshtaol (v. 2) are cities from the old Danite territory that were encountered in the Samson stories. The scouts probably recognized the Levite by his accent as coming from the south (v. 3). One of the primary roles of the priest was to consult God on behalf of the people (v. 5). The priest's favorable response will be used later to justify the conquest of Laish and the slaughter of its inhabitants (v. 10).

Laish (v. 7) was a city at the northern extremity of the land, near the sources of the Jordan River. The place is rich in resources, and the people, quiet and trusting, live in an unwalled city. The statement that the people lived "after the manner of the Sidonians" seems to indicate that the city followed Phoenician customs. The scouts justify their recommendation to attack the city by saying that God has given it into their power (vv. 8-10 and see v. 6). "Mahaneh-dan" (v. 12) means "camp of Dan."

The Danites put their little ones, their livestock, and their goods at the head of the column (v. 21) because they expect to be attacked from the rear as soon as Micah discovers that they have stolen his idols and priest. Micah

me? How, then, can you ask me what I want?" ²⁵The Danites said to him, "Let us hear no further sound from you, lest fierce men fall upon you and you and your family lose your lives." ²⁶The Danites then went on their way, and Micah, seeing that they were stronger than he, returned home.

²⁷Having taken what Micah had made, and the priest he had had, they attacked Laish, a quiet and trusting people; they put them to the sword and destroyed their city by fire. ²⁸No one came to their aid, since the city was far from Sidon and they had no contact with other people. The Danites then rebuilt the city, which was in the valley that belongs to Beth-rehob, and lived there. ²⁹They named it Dan after their ancestor Dan, son of Israel.

However, the name of the city was formerly Laish. ³⁰The Danites set up the carved idol for themselves, and Jonathan, son of Gershom, son of Moses, and his descendants were the priests for the tribe of the Danites until the time of the captivity of the land. ³¹They maintained the carved idol Micah had made as long as the house of God was in Shiloh.

19 **The Levite from Ephraim.** ¹At that time, when there was no king in Israel, there was a Levite residing in remote parts of the mountain region of Ephraim who had taken for himself a concubine for Bethlehem of Judah. ²His concubine was unfaithful to him and left him for her father's house in Bethlehem of Judah, where she stayed for some four months. ³Her husband then set out with

does chase after them but, when he discovers how strong a force they are, he returns home (vv. 22-26).

The slaughter of the people of Laish (v. 27) is unjustifiable. What sin has led to! The Danites rebuild the city, name it after their ancestor, and set up the carved idol that was Micah's (vv. 28-30). In verse 30 the Levite suddenly has a name, Jonathan, son of Gershom, son of Moses. The "time of the captivity of the land" (v. 30) refers to the year 734 B.C., when northern Palestine came under the Assyrians and the temple at Dan was destroyed. Verse 31 mentions that the Danites had preserved their sanctuary at Dan during the same time that the real house of God was at Shiloh (v. 31).

19:1–21:25 Civil war against Benjamin. These three chapters are made up of a number of originally independent narratives that have been skillfully combined into a continuous story. They present another example of how things could go wrong because "in those days there was no king in Israel; everyone did what he thought best" (21:25). A hideous crime is committed, and Israel so overreacts to it that they bring on a full-scale civil war.

These chapters fall into three scenes: the episode with the Levite and his concubine (19:1-30); the assembly of Israel and the resultant war against Benjamin (20:1-48); and the getting of wives for the surviving Benjaminites (21:1-25).

19:1-30 The Levite and his concubine. The story of the Levite who goes to Bethlehem to retrieve his wife, and who then suffers a gross indignity on his return, is told to explain why war breaks out between Benjamin and the

his servant and a pair of asses, and went after her to forgive her and take her back. She brought him into her father's house, and on seeing him, the girl's father joyfully made him welcome. ⁴He was detained by the girl's father, and so he spent three days with this father-in-law of his, eating and drinking and passing the night there. ⁵On the fourth day they rose early in the morning and he prepared to go. But the girl's father said to his son-in-law, "Fortify yourself with a little food; you can go later on." ⁶So they stayed and the two men ate and drank together. Then the girl's father said to the husband, "Why not decide to spend the night here and enjoy yourself?" ⁷The man still made a move to go, but when his father-in-law pressed him he went back and spent the night there.

⁸On the fifth morning he rose early to depart, but the girl's father said, "Fortify yourself and tarry until the afternoon." When he and his father-in-law had eaten, ⁹and the husband was ready to go with his concubine and servant, the girl's father said to him, "It is already growing dusk. Stay for the night. See, the day is coming to an end. Spend the night here and enjoy yourself. Early tomorrow you can start your journey home." ¹⁰The man, however, refused to stay another night; he and his concubine set out with a pair of saddled asses, and traveled till they came opposite Jebus, which is Jerusalem. ¹¹Since they were near Jebus with the day far gone, the servant said to his master, "Come, let us turn off to this city of the Jebusites and spend the night in it." ¹²But his master said to him, "We will not turn off to a city of foreigners, who are not Israelites, but will go on to Gibeah. ¹³Come," he said to his servant, "let us make for some other place, either Gibeah or Ramah, to spend the night." ¹⁴So they continued on their way till the sun set on them when they were abreast of Gibeah of Benjamin.

¹⁵There they turned off to enter Gibeah for the night. The man waited in the public square of the city he had entered, but no one offered them the shelter of his home for the night. ¹⁶In the evening, however, an old man came from his work in the field; he was from the mountain region of Ephraim, though he lived among the Benjaminite townspeople of Gibeah. ¹⁷When he noticed the traveler in the public square of the city, the old man asked where he was going, and

other tribes of Israel. The story is full of dramatic irony: the father-in-law's hospitality so delays the Levite's return that he cannot make the trip back home in one day; had he stopped in Jebus, the Canaanite city, he would have avoided the outrage; he is offered hospitality in Gibeah, not by a Benjaminite but by another sojourner.

That the man is a Levite is not important for the purpose of the story. Though the editor identifies "Jebus" as "Jerusalem" (v. 10), Jerusalem, in fact, never bore that name. Perhaps Jebus was a suburb of Jerusalem. At this time Jerusalem was still a Canaanite city. Gibeah was about three miles north of Jerusalem, and Ramah was about two miles further north.

Entering Gibeah, the Levite receives no offers of hospitality from the Benjaminites there, but is taken in by another stranger, an old man who, like the Levite, also came from the mountain region of Ephraim. The old man shows the Levite the same hospitality that his father-in-law had shown him

whence he had come. ¹⁸He said to him, "We are traveling from Bethlehem of Judah far up into the mountain region of Ephraim, where I belong. I have been to Bethlehem of Judah and am now going back home; but no one has offered us the shelter of his house. ¹⁹We have straw and fodder for our asses, and bread and wine for the woman and myself and for our servant; there is nothing else we need." ²⁰"You are welcome," the old man said to him, "but let me provide for all your needs, and do not spend the night in the public square." ²¹So he led them to his house and provided fodder for the asses. Then they washed their feet, and ate and drank.

The Outrage at Gibeah. ²²While they were enjoying themselves, the men of the city, who were corrupt, surrounded the house and beat on the door. They said to the old man whose house it was, "Bring out your guest, that we may abuse him." ²³The owner of the house went out to them and said, "No, my brothers; do not be so wicked. Since this man is my guest, do not commit this crime. ²⁴Rather let me bring out my maiden daughter or his concubine. Ravish them, or do whatever you want with them; but against the man you must not commit this wanton crime." ²⁵When the men would not listen to his host, the husband seized his concubine

and thrust her outside to them. They had relations with her and abused her all night until the following dawn, when they let her go. ²⁶Then at daybreak the woman came and collapsed at the entrance of the house in which her husband was a guest, where she lay until the morning. ²⁷When her husband rose that day and opened the door of the house to start out again on his journey, there lay the woman, his concubine, at the entrance of the house with her hands on the threshold. ²⁸He said to her, "Come, let us go"; but there was no answer. So the man placed her on an ass and started out again for home.

²⁹On reaching home, he took a knife to the body of his concubine, cut her into twelve pieces, and sent them throughout the territory of Israel. ³⁰Everyone who saw this said, "Nothing like this has been done or seen from the day the Israelites came up from the land of Egypt to this day. Take note of it, and state what you propose to do."

20 **Assembly of Israelites.** ¹So all the Israelites came out as one man: from Dan to Beer-sheba, and from the land of Gilead, the community was gathered to the LORD at Mizpah. ²The leaders of all the people and all the tribesmen of Israel, four hundred thousand foot soldiers who were swordsmen, presented themselves in the assembly of

in Bethlehem. The verb "abuse" in verse 22 is an attempt to translate the Hebrew verb that means "to know," a verb used euphemistically in the Old Testament to denote sexual intercourse. It is used here in a deliberately ambiguous way.

The gruesome act of cutting up the dead woman and sending pieces of her to all the tribes serves the purpose of arousing the tribes against Gibeah for the outrage they have committed (see 1 Sam 11:7). The implication is that the tribes must help the Levite take revenge on Gibeah or suffer a like fate.

20:1-48 War against Benjamin. In response to the call of the Levite the Israelites gather at Mizpah, about eight miles north of Jerusalem (vv. 1-2). "Dan to Beer-sheba" is a phrase that represents the northern and southern boundaries of ancient Israel. The Israelites on the eastern side of the Jordan

the people of God. ³Meanwhile, the Benjaminites heard that the Israelites had gone up to Mizpah. The Israelites asked to be told how the crime had taken place, ⁴and the Levite, the husband of the murdered woman, testified: "My concubine and I went into Gibeah of Benjamin for the night. ⁵But the citizens of Gibeah rose up against me by night and surrounded the house in which I was. Me they attempted to kill, and my concubine they abused so that she died. ⁶So I took my concubine and cut her up and sent her through every part of the territory of Israel, because of the monstrous crime they had committed in Israel. ⁷Now that you are all here, O Israelites, state what you propose to do." ⁸All the people rose as one man to say, "None of us is to leave for his tent or return to his home. ⁹Now as for Gibeah, this is what we will do: We will proceed against it by lot, ¹⁰taking from all the tribes of Israel ten men for every hundred, a hundred for every thousand, a thousand for every ten thousand, and procuring supplies for the soldiers who will go to deal fully and suitably with Gibeah of Benjamin for the crime it committed in Israel."

¹¹When, therefore, all the men of Israel without exception were leagued together against the city, ¹²the tribes of Israel sent men throughout the tribe of Benjamin to say, "What is this evil which has occurred among you? ¹³Now give up these corrupt men of Gibeah, that we may put them to death and thus purge the evil from Israel." But the Benjaminites refused to accede to the demand of their brothers, the Israelites. ¹⁴Instead, the Benjaminites assembled from their other cities to Gibeah, to do battle with the Israelites. ¹⁵The number of the Benjaminite swordsmen from the other cities on that occasion was twenty-six thousand, in addition to the inhabitants of Gibeah. ¹⁶Included in this total were seven hundred picked men who were left-handed, every one of them able to sling a stone at a hair without missing. ¹⁷Meanwhile the other Israelites who, without Benjamin, mustered four hundred thousand swordsmen ready for battle, ¹⁸moved on to Bethel and consulted God. When the Israelites asked who should go first in the attack on the Benjaminites, the Lᴏʀᴅ said, "Judah shall go first." ¹⁹The next day the Israelites advanced on Gibeah with their forces.

War with Benjamin. ²⁰On the day the Israelites drew up in battle array in Gibeah for the combat with Benjamin, ²¹the Benjaminites came out of the city and felled twenty-two thousand men of Israel. ²³Then the Israelites went up and wept before the Lᴏʀᴅ until evening. "Shall I again engage my brother Benjamin in battle?" they asked the Lᴏʀᴅ; and the

River (land of Gilead) also come to the assembly. The size of the armies (vv. 8-10) is exaggerated. Perhaps the Hebrew word for "thousand" refers to a particular military grouping or contingent, as we saw in the Book of Joshua.

In verse 16 the narrator seems to suggest that one reason why the Benjaminites will endure and be able to inflict great losses on the Israelites is because of the seven hundred sharpshooters. The Israelites go over to Bethel, a few miles away, to consult the Lord on who should attack first. The lot falls to Judah (vv. 17-19).

The first two attacks against Gibeah are repulsed, and the Israelites suffer some significant losses (vv. 20-25). After the second loss the Israelites

LORD answered that they should. ²²But though the Israelite soldiers took courage and again drew up for combat in the same place as on the previous day, ²⁴when they met the Benjaminites for the second time, ²⁵once again the Benjaminites who came out of Gibeah against them felled eighteen thousand Israelites, all of them swordsmen. ²⁶So the entire Israelite army went up to Bethel, where they wept and remained fasting before the LORD until evening of that day, besides offering holocausts and peace offerings before the LORD. ²⁷When the Israelites consulted the LORD (for the ark of the covenant of God was there in those days, ²⁸and Phinehas, son of Eleazar, son of Aaron, was ministering to him in those days), and asked, "Shall I go out again to battle with Benjamin, my brother, or shall I desist?" The LORD said, "Attack! for tommorrow I will deliver him into your power." ²⁹So Israel set men in ambush around Gibeah.

³⁰The Israelites went up against the Benjaminites for the third time and formed their line of battle at Gibeah as on other occasions. ³¹The Benjaminites went out to meet them, and in the beginning they killed off about thirty of the Israelite soldiers in the open field, just as on the other occasions. ³²Therefore the Benjaminites thought, "We are defeating them as before," not realizing that disaster was about to overtake them. The Israelites, however, had planned the flight so as to draw them away from the city onto the highways. They were drawn away from the city onto the highways, of which the one led to Bethel, the other to Gibeon. ³³And then all the men of

Israel rose from their places. They reformed their ranks at Baal-tamar, and the Israelites in ambush rushed from their place west of Gibeah, ³⁴ten thousand picked men from all Israel, and advanced against the city itself. In a fierce battle, ³⁵the LORD defeated Benjamin before Israel; and on that day the Israelites killed twenty-five thousand one hundred men of Benjamin, all of them swordsmen.

³⁶To the Benjaminites it had looked as though the enemy were defeated, for the men of Israel gave ground to Benjamin, trusting in the ambush they had set at Gibeah. ³⁷But then the men in ambush made a sudden dash into Gibeah, overran it, and put the whole city to the sword. ³⁸Now, the other Israelites had agreed with the men in ambush on a smoke signal they were to send up from the city. ³⁹And though the men of Benjamin had begun by killing off some thirty of the men of Israel, under the impression that they were defeating them as surely as in the earlier fighting, the Israelites wheeled about to resist ⁴⁰as the smoke of the signal column began to rise up from the city. It was when Benjamin looked back and saw the whole city in flames against the sky ⁴¹that the men of Israel wheeled about. Therefore the men of Benjamin were thrown into confusion, for they realized the disaster that had overtaken them. ⁴²They retreated before the men of Israel in the direction of the desert, with the fight being pressed against them. In their very midst, meanwhile, those who had been in the city were spreading destruction. ⁴³The men of Benjamin had been surrounded, and were now pursued

consult the Lord, they fast, and offer holocausts and peace offerings (vv. 26-27). This time they are told that they will be successful because the Lord will deliver the Benjaminites into their power (v. 28).

Verses 29-43 are two accounts, clumsily combined, of the same event. The account in verses 29-36 describes more the field tactics of the troops, while the account in verses 37-43 describes the victory from the perspective

to a point east of Gibeah, ⁴⁴while eighteen thousand of them fell, warriors to a man. ⁴⁵The rest turned and fled through the desert to the rock Rimmon. But on the highways the Israelites picked off five thousand men among them, and chasing them up to Gidom, killed another two thousand of them there. ⁴⁶Those of Benjamin who fell on that day were in all twenty-five thousand swordsmen, warriors to a man. ⁴⁷But six hundred others who turned and fled through the desert reached the rock Rimmon, where they remained for four months.

⁴⁸The men of Israel withdrew through the territory of the Benjaminites, putting to the sword the inhabitants of the cities, the livestock, and all they chanced upon. Moreover they destroyed by fire all the cities they came upon.

21 **Wives for the Survivors.** ¹Now the men of Israel had sworn at Mizpah that none of them would give his daughter in marriage to anyone from Benjamin. ²So the people went to Bethel and remained there before God until evening, raising their voices in bitter lament. ³They said, "LORD, God of Israel, why has it come to pass in Israel that today one tribe of Israel should be lacking?" ⁴Early the next day the people built an altar there and offered holocausts and peace offerings. ⁵Then the Israelites asked, "Are there any among all the tribes of Israel who did not come up to the LORD for the assembly?" For they had taken a solemn oath that anyone who did not go up to the LORD at Mizpah should be put to death without fail.

⁶The Israelites were disconsolate over their brother Benjamin and said, "Today one of the tribes of Israel has been cut off. ⁷What can we do about wives for the survivors, since we have sworn by the LORD not to give them any of our daughters in marriage?" ⁸And when they asked whether anyone among the tribes of Israel had not come up to the LORD in Mizpah, they found that none of the men of Jabesh-gilead had come to the encampment for the assembly. ⁹A roll call of the army established that none of the inhabitants of that city were present. ¹⁰The community, therefore, sent twelve thousand warriors with orders to go to Jabesh-gilead and put those who lived there to the sword, including the women and children. ¹¹They were told to include under the ban all males and every woman who was not still a virgin. ¹²Finding among the inhabitants of Jabesh-gilead four hundred young virgins, who had had no relations with men, they brought them to the camp at Shiloh in the land of Canaan. ¹³Then the whole community sent a message to the Benjaminites at the rock

of the successful ambush. Both have a resemblance to the capture of Ai in Josh 8. Notice that in verse 35 it is the Lord who defeats Benjamin. Verses 44-48 give the statistics on the fallen. In the end there remain only 600, who escape to the rock Rimmon (v. 47). The location of Rimmon is unknown. Though the tradition of war against Benjamin may be early, the story as we have it here has been revised to make it fit. The original tradition probably dealt with a war between Benjamin and its northern neighbor, Ephraim. It is unlikely that such a near obliteration of a tribe ever occurred.

21:1-25 Wives for the Benjaminites. Having almost wiped out an entire tribe, the Israelites realize that if that tribe is going to survive they must obtain wives for the six hundred male survivors. This chapter presents two accounts of how they obtained wives. The separate accounts have been har-

Rimmon, offering them peace. ¹⁴When Benjamin returned at that time, they gave them as wives the women of Jabesh-gilead whom they had spared; but these proved to be not enough for them.

¹⁵The people were still disconsolate over Benjamin because the Lᴏʀᴅ had made a breach among the tribes of Israel. ¹⁶And the elders of the community said, "What shall we do for wives for the survivors? For every woman in Benjamin has been put to death." ¹⁷They said, "Those of Benjamin who survive must have heirs, else one of the Israelite tribes will be wiped out. ¹⁸Yet we cannot give them any of our daughters in marriage, because the Israelites have sworn, 'Cursed be he who gives a woman to Benjamin!' " ¹⁹Then they thought of the yearly feast of the Lᴏʀᴅ at Shiloh, north of Bethel, east of the highway that goes up from Bethel to Shechem, and south of Lebonah. ²⁰And they instructed the Benjaminites, "Go and lie in wait in the vineyards. ²¹When you see the girls of Shiloh come out to do their dancing, leave the vineyards and each of you seize one of the girls of Shiloh for a wife, and go to the land of Benjamin. ²²When their fathers or their brothers come to complain to us, we shall say to them, 'Release them to us as a kindness, since we did not take a woman apiece in the war. Had you yourselves given them these wives, you would now be guilty.' "

²³The Benjaminites did this; they carried off a wife for each of them from their raid on the dancers, and went back to their own territory, where they rebuilt and occupied the cities. ²⁴Also at that time the Israelites dispersed; each of them left for his own heritage in his own clan and tribe.

²⁵In those days there was no king in Israel; everyone did what he thought best.

monized by the explanation that each stratagem provided only a partial solution to the problem (v. 14).

The first account (vv. 1-14) states the underlying problem, namely, that at Mizpah the men of Israel had sworn that none of them would give their daughters in marriage to anyone from Benjamin (v. 1). The solution that they eventually hit upon is to see if anyone had not come up for the assembly, since a solemn oath had been taken that anyone who did not come up would be put to death (vv. 2-5). Jabesh-gilead was east of the Jordan.

The second stratagem has parallels in Roman and Greek folklore (vv. 15-23). The elders remember the yearly feast at Shiloh when the girls of Shiloh came out to dance. Each Benjaminite is told to seize one of them for a wife. The elders promise to intercede for the Benjaminites when the fathers or brothers of the girls complain. Because they have been stolen from them, not given to the Benjaminites, the men of Shiloh will not be guilty of breaking their vow not to give their daughters in marriage to a Benjaminite (v. 22). The great assembly, called in 20:1, is now dispersed and the Israelites return to their own heritage (v. 24).

The narrator concludes by saying again that all these sad goings-on took place because "in those days there was no king in Israel; everyone did what he thought best" (v. 25). Israel's history of sin has begun. Eventually that sinfulness will lead to the destruction of the northern kingdom of Israel in the eighth century and the destruction of the southern kingdom of Judah in the sixth century. However, the book has pointed out more than once not only the saving power of the Lord, but also the Lord's will to save the Israelites when they cry out to the Lord.

REVIEW AIDS AND DISCUSSION TOPICS

I

Joshua: Introduction (pages 5–8)

1. What books are included in the "Deuteronomistic History," and how was this work formed?
2. What was the historical context for writing the Deuteronomistic History, and what was its purpose?
3. In the context of the Deuteronomistic History what was the purpose of the Book of Joshua? Does the message of the Book of Joshua have any meaning for us today?
4. Is the Book of Joshua historically accurate? What was the author's major concern in telling the story of the occupation of the land?

II

Josh 1:1–12:24 The Conquest (pages 9–37)

1. What is meant by an "etiology" (see 2:1-24; 4:1-9; 8:24-29; 9:1-27)?
2. How is Joshua compared to Moses, and what is the point of this comparison (see 1:10-18; 3:7; 4:14; 8:10-23)?
3. What is the prism through which the crossing of the Jordan is understood, and what is the point of the comparison (see 3:14-17; 4:20-24; 5:2-12)?
4. How does the author convey the message of the book to the exiles (see 1:1-9; 3:1-13; 4:1-9; 6:6-27; 10:8-14 and 25; 11:16-23; 21:43-45)?
5. What was the basic point of the story about Ai (7:1–8:29)?

III

Josh 13:1–22:34 The Division of the Land (pages 37–55)

1. What was the origin of the materials used in this section of the book?
2. What was the purpose of these chapters?
3. What was the purpose of the cities of asylum (20:1-9)?
4. What seems to stand behind the list of Levitical cities (21:1-42)?

IV

Josh 23:1–24:33 Joshua's Farewell and Death (pages 55–60)

1. What is the background for understanding these two chapters?
2. What is the purpose of 23:1-16?
3. Is there a historical basis to chapter 24?
4. What is the purpose of chapter 24, and what does it have to say to us?

V

Judges: Introduction (pages 61–63)

1. Who were the judges?

117

2. What is the purpose of the Book of Judges in the context of the Deuteronomistic History?

3. What was the origin of the stories of the judges, and how accurate are they historically?

4. What are the elements of the theological framework that has been imposed upon the stories of the major judges? What is the message for the exiles (see 2:11-19) and for us?

VI

Judg 1:1-2:5 The Conquest (pages 64-67)

1. How does the story of the conquest in the Book of Judges differ from the account in the Book of Joshua?

2. How does chapter 1 relate to 2:1-5 and what was the message in this material for the exiles?

VII

Judg 2:6-16:31 The Judges (pages 67-104)

1. What is involved in Israel's cry to the Lord (see 2:18 and 10:6-16)?

2. What is the relationship between chapters 4 and 5? What point did they make to the exiles?

3. What is the new element in the story of Gideon (see 6:7-10) and what message did it have for the exiles?

4. In the story of Gideon, who is responsible for Israel's victory over the Midianites?

5. How does the story of Abimelech differ from the other stories in the Book of Judges? What is the view of the monarchy presented in the story?

6. What is the importance of 10:6-16 in the Book of Judges? What is the message of these verses for the exiles and for us?

7. How is one to explain the apparent acceptance of human sacrifice in 11:29-40?

8. How are Samson's exploits to be viewed in terms of a deliverance of Israel from oppression?

VIII

Judg 17:1-21:25 Appendix (pages 104-115)

1. What view toward the monarchy did the editor who inserted this material have?

2. What was the point of the story about the migration of the tribe of Dan (chapters 17-18)?

3. What was the point of the story of the war against Benjamin (chapters 19-21)?

DIVISION OF CANAAN

Miles 0 — 40
Kms 0 — 40

MEDITERRANEAN

SEA

SIDONIANS

LEBANON MTS.

HITTITES

ARAMEANS

Sidon

Damascus

MT. HERMON

Tyre

DAN

Dan (Laish)

ASHER

NAPHTALI

Hazor

MANASSEH (EAST)

MT. CARMEL

Lake Galilee

Ashtaroth

ZEBULUN

MT. TABOR

Endor

Dor

Megiddo

Shunem

ISSACHAR

Jezreel

MT. GILBOA

Ramoth

MANASSEH (WEST)

Jordan River

Jabesh

Shechem

GAD

AMMONITES

Joppa

Shiloh

EPHRAIM

Bethel

Gilgal

Rabbah

DAN

Ai

BENJAMIN

Jericho

Ashdod

Gibeah

Jerusalem

Bethpeor

Libnah

Bethlehem

Ashkelon

REUBEN

PHILISTINES

Gath?

Lachish

JUDAH

Hebron

Dead

Gaza

Engedi

Sea

Gath?

MOABITES

Beersheba

Hormah

SIMEON

The Negev

EDOMITES

© United Bible Societies, 1976